style your life
by Julia Dawn

Style Your Life

ISBN: 978-1-63493-216-5 (trade paperback)
ISBN: 978-1-63493-217-2 (e-book)

For questions, please contact:
Access Consciousness Publishing
406 Present Street
Stafford, TX 77477 USA
accessconsciousnesspublishing.com

Illustrations: Simran Bhui

All products, services and information provided by the author are for general education and entertainment purposes only.

To,

My father for showing me that the world is to soar and not just to survive. Thank you for being the most phenomenal papa and giving me a space for me to step up and know I can go wherever I want to, do whatever I want to, without having to give any answers and explanations. Thank you for always having my back, asking me what happened when you saw no smile on my face and just sitting and cracking stupid jokes in those moments that made me crack up so much, for letting me follow my dreams without having any kind of judgment of what I was doing, or how I was doing it. Thank you for being my friend, for inspiring me, for being my motivation, for making me realize that there's so much that's possible, for never asking me to slow down or increase my pace. Thank you for just being there papa. You were and always will be my hero! You are my strength! Your kindness, and selflessness are treasures.

I love you papa

Acknowledgment

There are so many beautiful people who are a special part of my life and continue to contribute hugely in their own magnificent ways.

To start with, thank you to my beautiful mother for being my support, for asking me questions, for being in allowance of me in all the moments I required it. Thank you for being my mama and always showing me that truly there is so much more possible! I love you mom and I love creating miracles with you! You inspire me more and more every day! Thank you for choosing greater, I admire you.

My beautiful sister, Nooru thank you for adding the magic of you in my life. Thank you for always being blunt and saying things as they are and being my confidante and my 3am buddy. I love you my Noora! Thank you for choosing me as your sister, I got really lucky bro!

A big thank you to Ooty veerjee (Rattan D Singh) and Kiran Massi (Kiran Singh) to have empowered me to see my magic and choose way greater than what I had decided I was to live. You guys changed my life! Thank you! I love you both very much.

Big thank you to Tulika (Tulika Singh) for being my friend! I have learned so much from you. Thank you for always having my back. Above all thank you for always choosing greater and being such a huge inspiration to choose greater and greater. I love you very much!

Huge thank you to my very special Smriti Aunty (Smriti Shivdesani) for being the elegance, beauty and loving energy that you are and showering it into all our lives. Thank you for always having my back. I love you!!

My bunch of friends, I could not have written this without you guys constantly kicking me every time I judged myself! From the insane laughter, the no brainer conversations with you all to the heavy duty "I've got you" conversations, they all make my world a very happy place! I really do have the greatest and the best friends, I know I asked for ;). I love each one of you so so much. Each one of you inspires me to be greater than yesterday! How does it truly get better?

Last but not the least, Gary and Dain, thank you for being you! You empower so many of us around the world to ask for greater change and show us that we don't have to "settle".

ISHA BAWA

Thank you for showing me the beauty in me!

Life has not been the same and will not be. ;)

What else is possible® now?

FASHION IS NOT SOMETHING THAT
EXISTS IN DRESSES ONLY. FASHION IS IN
THE SKY, IN THE STREET, FASHION HAS TO
DO WITH IDEAS, THE WAY WE LIVE, WHAT
IS HAPPENING.

Coco Chanel

Contents

Introduction...9

Being In Question...11

Chapter 1: On Life and Living................................19

Chapter 2: On Style..29

Chapter 3: On Embracing The Moment.................35

Chapter 4: On Power..45

Chapter 5: On Beauty...55

Chapter 6: On Bodies...63

Chapter 7: Your Wardrobe Workout.......................81

Chapter 8: On Wealth...87

Chapter 9: On Actualizing With Energy Pulls.......101

Chapter 10: On Colours 123

Chapter 11: Handy Tips...135

Chapter 12: Styling Your Future...........................139

All Clearings...143

About The Author..163

About Access Consciousness® 166

Introduction

First of all, welcome to Style Your Life, you beautiful being. Thank you for choosing to step into a space of choosing to see what creates greater for you. Before we begin, I would love to say that Style Your Life is not about changing you or making you into someone else. Style Your Life is about destroying all the points of view you have that limit you from being the phenomenance you are seeking to be, with the help of all the amazing tools of Access Consciousness®! Here's something I have to tell you that'll probably burst your bubble, or not ;), you cannot see something in someone else or perceive to be something if you aren't already it! So there you go, everything you want to be, everything you want to see yourself as – you already are it! You just have to choose to acknowledge it ☺.

What would you like your life to look like? What if you could style your life? If there was no past to define you or what you've done or what has been done to you, what would your life be like? What would you like to style your life as? If there were no limitations, what would you style your life as? What would you style your body as, your relationships as, your business as?

Are you willing to let your life and world be styled by you, not by your circumstances, not by others, not by the limitations that have been put on you.

What if you could style your life?

I studied fashion for 4 years. I realized the fashion world had a lot of judgments to it (to be subtle). After being introduced to the tools of Access, I've always been in question of how fashion, style, and clothing can be embraced for the beauty it is without having so many judgments, agendas, and without focusing on perfection.

This book is a new perspective of what fashion is and what style can be, with the help of the phenomenal tools of Access Consciousness®.

Being In Question

"The gift of our curiosity is its power to open us up to new and greater possibility in every moment. Curiosity is essentially the state of being in constant, unhindered question, inquiry and wonder.

Discussions around the psychological benefits of curiosity indicate that not only is it key to creating lasting happiness, it also has the power to change your life and the world around you. Even Einstein, one of the greatest minds of our time, credited his curiosity above his talent or intellect.

One of the most dynamic ways we impair our curiosity is when we judge, self-criticize, or see any part of our lives or ourselves as lacking.

Questions are a simple yet dynamic catalyst for creating change. Asking the right questions will re-ignite curiosity, and allow you to explore your difference, capacities, greatness and your possibilities that you have been hiding behind all those judgments, conclusions and limiting beliefs."

Dr. Dain Heer.

One of the first tools discussed is to be in the question. A question always empowers you and an answer will always disempower you.

The thing with an answer is that it only leads to closed doors and shuts all open doors. A question will create a possibility; it will open a new door that you thought never existed.

For example, if you ask "How does it get any better than this?®" when something good happens, it gets better and when you ask it when something bad happens, it gets better but if you go into the conclusion of how horrible things are you'll never be able to change it!

The Clearing Statement

What if a few weird words could totally change your life? Access Consciousness® offers potent tools for change and transformation. If you are around people who have done Access Consciousness® classes or tele-calls, you are likely to hear them say this weird thing that sounds totally like a foreign language, or maybe you won't even hear it because your brain has just turned into mush! (In case you're wondering… this is a really good thing – it means the clearing statement is working its magic on you!).

Whenever you're willing to destroy and uncreate and let go of something that is limiting you, it instantly opens up the space for something less limited or even unlimited to show up." – Gary Douglas

These crazy weird words are the Access Consciousness® Clearing Statement – a simple tool that thousands of people around the world use every day to continually create a life of ease, joy and glory.

It goes like this:

"Right and Wrong, Good and Bad, POC and POD, All 9, Shorts, Boys and Beyonds®".

You can use it to change almost anything that is keeping you stuck, limited or tied up in knots!

How Does The Clearing Statement Work?

Much of what we would like to change is not cognitive or logical; it is created and held energetically. Take a moment to recall a time when you got really angry about something without being clear about the logical reason… was it actually an energy you were aware of?

Many modalities clear the limitations built around words. Access Consciousness® clears the energy underneath the words.

The beauty, magic and potency of the Access Consciousness® Clearing Statement is its capacity to clear the hidden stuff that you aren't even aware of that is keeping you stuck! So, you don't need to go through the pain, suffering and gory of reliving a situation to clear the charge on it. How does it get even better than that?

When you ask a question or think about something that is limiting you or not working for you, there is an energy that comes up. It's a lot like defragging a computer. The energy comes up, you run the clearing statement and then you have a whole lot more space from which to create anything you choose.

The Clearing Statement Explained

This is what the shorthand stands for:

Right and Wrong, Good and Bad

What's good, perfect and correct about this?

What's wrong, mean, vicious, terrible, bad, and awful about this?

What's right and wrong, good and bad?

POC

Is the point of creation of the thoughts, feelings and emotions immediately preceding whatever you decided.

POD

Is the point of destruction immediately following whatever you decided. It's like pulling the bottom card out of a house of cards. The whole thing falls down.

All 9

Stands for nine layers of crap that we're taking out. You know that somewhere in those nine layers, there's got to be a pony because you couldn't put that much crap in one place without having a pony in there. It's crap that you're generating yourself, which is the bad part. You created it, you can change it.

Shorts

Is the short version of: What's meaningful about this? What's meaningless about this? What's the punishment for this? What's the reward for this?

Boys

Stands for nucleated spheres. Have you ever been told you have to peel the layers of the onion to get to the core of an issue? Well, this is it—except it's not an onion. It's an energetic structure that looks like one. These are pre-verbal.

Have you ever seen one of those kids' bubble pipes? Blow here and you create a mass of bubbles on the other end of the pipe? As you pop one bubble it fills back in. Basically these have to do with those areas of our life where we've tried to change something continuously with no effect. This is what keeps something repeating ad infinitum…

Beyonds

Are feelings or sensations you get that stop your heart, stop your breath, or stop your willingness to look at possibilities. It's like when your business is in the red and you get another final notice and you say argh! You weren't expecting that right now.

And sometimes we just say, "POC and POD it."

(Taken from http://drdainheer.com/free-stuff/the-clearing-statement/)

Chapter 1

On Life and Living

"LIFE IS A PARTY. DRESS FOR IT."

Audrey Hepburn

When we talk about life, everything suddenly becomes serious and sense of humor flies out of the window. What if life was actually a party? A party where you have fun, where you have so much fun that it doesn't matter who watches you and who doesn't. Do you know why? Because you are too busy laughing, sharing jokes, dancing, crying even, just because YOU feel like it.

When you say "I have a great life", you have already concluded that life has ended. It has an energy of "one day it'll end", so you've decided that there is a stop point. What if instead of that you could call it your living?

Are you living your life like a party or like a party pooper? There's no harm in being a party pooper as long as you know and realize that once you're done being it you can still stand up and throw a party! Okay, before we move on have you told yourself that you don't like parties? Let me ask you a question, what have you defined a party as? 300 people, drunk nights, socializing with people you wouldn't want to talk to, being asked questions you don't want to answer to? Woah, okay All the definitions you've given to partying can you destroy and uncreate that?" ***Right and wrong, good and bad, pod and poc, all 9, shorts, boys and beyonds®.***

What if having fun could be called a party? For me, every time I have fun I am partying, every time I laugh my life is a celebration- a celebration of who I am, and who I be. Are you willing to celebrate you every second of your living? Are you willing to ask for that to show up? Everything that doesn't allow that can we destroy and uncreate that? ***Right and wrong, good and bad, pod and poc, all 9, shorts, boys and beyonds®.***

What lies, whose lies and how many lies are you using to create mourning as your life are you choosing?

Style your Life

Right and wrong, good and bad, pod and poc, all 9, shorts, boys and beyonds®.

What stops us from celebrating our life is a lot to do with our definitions of what our life should look like, what we should look like, our expectations of ourselves and how many of those that haven't been met. What about all that you aren't looking at? All those beautiful creations of yours, all those moments you brought a smile to someone else's face, all those moments someone got inspired by you, by something you said or just were being that allowed them to be their brilliance? Is that not your brilliance? Oh, sweet beings you are brilliance walking, talking and being. Is it time you acknowledge that now? You could, or you could hold onto it ☺.

As a child, I was someone who was looked at as shy, closed, even weak, among lots of other things. Oh, the joy of labels ;). I wasn't shy and weak, oh dear no fucking way. What I know I was, was that I was an energy of softness and kindness that was looked upon as weakness in this very reality. My strength was and is my softness, my willingness to be different! There was a beautiful teacher in grade 5 who saw me, saw my brilliance, encouraged me to be greater, not by changing who I was but by embracing all of it, all of me. I had the confidence to smile in her classes, ask questions and get awesome grades. What had changed? Not me, what had changed was a perspective, towards me and for that I will always be grateful. But this is what we do every moment, we wait for someone to see us, to show us our potential so we can finally celebrate ourselves, finally stand with our universe expanded and not contracted, stand with the knowing that someone has our back. What if we don't need someone to have our back? What if the universe has our back in every moment of every day? Yes, it does, yes it sees you, yes it knows your greatness. Are you willing for it to show it to you? The universe is dying to play with you in this celebration, are you going to ask it to join you? Ask and Receive my beautiful friends. You shall receive all you desire if you ask! Let's ask the universe in this very moment "Hey universe! Thank you for having my back even in those moments I thought you didn't and every time I refused the gifts you wanted me to have. I am willing to receive all you would like to gift me. Thank you for having my back at all times, I ask you to show me the phenomenance I am and the phenomenance I am capable of creating. I will have it now! Thank You and I am so grateful for you." Woah, is that a different space? The universe always has your back guys, but it won't give you anything you're not willing to have. So, ask! Ask and have the trust that the universe will give you all you desire and greater.

Wrongness isn't a great colour on you

How much of your life have you spent being wrong? Little, a lot or megatons? Do you enjoy it? Does it give you pleasure or does it create less? What if you were never wrong, ever? What if it was other people's projections? And just because someone else has an awesomely hideous opinion on what you should do doesn't make it right and you wrong my friends. As the very beautiful and phenomenal Dr. Dain Heer and Gary Douglas have said "Others only accuse you of doing what they themselves are doing, every time someone judges you they aren't judging you, they are judging themselves and you would make yourselves wrong to give into their own satisfaction for what good reason?".

So, everything you have done to make yourself wrong and less to make others greater even though you knew you weren't wrong will you destroy and uncreate that? *Right and wrong, good and bad, pod and poc, all 9, shorts, boys and beyonds®.*

Whose lies, what lies and how many lies are you using to justify being wrong are you choosing?

Right and wrong, good and bad, pod and poc, all 9, shorts, boys and beyonds®.

You, my friend are not wrong, even though you think you are, even though you would like to take all the blame on yourself. "Only if I had done it differently, only if I had not said it." Oh my beauty, what if that was exactly what was required to be said and done in that moment? What if it created greater, not in the way you thought it would, in a way the universe knew it would. What if you losing your job was what was required for you to step up? What if you saying what you did was required for the next person to take action and step into their power? This takes me to one of my favourite tools of Access Consciousness®, asking "What's right about this I'm not getting?" "What's right about me I'm not getting?". Ask this even when you feel there is no one more pathetic than you are! I shall burst your bubble, nothing about you is pathetic. You are phenomenance, even when you buy the act of being anything else!

On that note here's a fun exercise that can help shift that energy of wrongness, self doubt and judgment. Enjoy!

Step 1

Write down a list of everything you think you are wrong for, everywhere you doubt yourself and your capacities, criticize yourself thoroughly. You're welcome ☺. I know you all enjoy it, sometimes. Don't stop and judge if you're getting it accurately or correctly. Just write it whether it's something your boss told you, your friend said for your own good (we all know that one), the unkind words that came out of someone's mouth, something someone said which they didn't "mean" to say. Don't make yourself wrong for it. Go ahead and jot it down.

Step 2

Look at it, be present with it, indulge in it. Cry if you feel like crying, scream if you want to, be present with it. Recognize that it will eventually pass away but for now because it's so valuable, be with it, acknowledge its value. Don't resist it, not anymore. Let it in. Feel every molecule of yours that has been implanted with the lie of you being wrong.

Step 3- Ask

Is this true for me right now?

Is it true sometimes? What happens just before it becomes true?

Did you make it true in the past and no longer has any energy in the present?

Step 4

Ask "Where did I buy that lie from?". The idea is not to go back in the past and dwell over it and make others wrong. It is just to realize that it was never yours to start with. And then ask "What lies, whose lies and how many lies am I using to create this as my reality am I choosing? *Right and wrong, good and bad, pod and poc, all 9, shorts, boys and beyonds®."*

Step 5

Continue being present with what's going on. After step 4 if there is still wrongness in your universe, ask for the wrongness to show up, even those that you are trying to hide. Look at the molecules, look at them and now start turning them 30 degrees, 60 degrees, 90 degrees, continue to be present, 180 degrees and then 360 degrees. Turn the molecules and now throw all the wrongness out of your world, throw it out completely. BOOM!

Step 6- Ask

What is possible for me now that wasn't possible 10 seconds ago? What am I unwilling to be and receive that if I would, could change my entire reality?

Chapter 2

On Style

"STYLE; ALL WHO HAVE IT HAVE ONE THING: ORIGINALITY."

Diana Vreeland

According to google, style is a particular procedure by which something is done; a manner or way. I'd like to ask you what is the particular way of living? Is there a particular way of living? I don't think so! For lots of people style is a particular way of dressing and being. I'm here to tell you style is however you would like to be, however you'd like to change. You know why? Because that might be your style ;) Being irrational and not predictable, having one set way of being.

Style is not something you look up the internet for. Yes, there are style tips but if you end up implementing those tips without asking if that's what is "you", you are not being style! Style is the essence of who you be. Having said that, you don't have to have just one style. Considering your energy is shifting every second, you are not being who you were yesterday so how can your style be constant? What if you didn't have to have one style statement? How much of your style is what you've decided you are and what you've defined yourself as? Are you ready to step beyond all definitions?

You have identities that you have created. When you create an identity, is that you, or is it a pretense of you? The problem is that you buy that identity as you. Identity never works very well because you always have to protect it and sell it and show everybody else that it's right and real and true and use a lot of energy to prove that the lies you created about you are true. How many of us create our personality and ourselves in totality based on our name? So many times it's almost like our job to defend for our name and stand up to the name that's been given to us. For example, Mahanveer means the mighty and brave warrior. So, someone with that name would probably feel the need to always be at war- with himself, with others and with everything around him. Similarly, if someone's name meant "pure", they would probably destroy themselves but never give up the point of view of being pure. Now who's setting the benchmark and definition of purity huh? I'm not saying this is the case for everyone, but it sure is a possibility. You have defined who and what you are and you are defending who and what you are as though that's the only thing you have available. There is a whole other universe that exists for us if we don't do defense. Every time you define you as black, white, straight, gay, male, or female, all of those definitions become what you then have to defend always, rather than: "I am an infinite being and I can choose anything I want." We have defined who or what we will receive and who or what we have to be. So the universe cannot contribute to you. Be aware of what people can receive and only give them the parts of you they can receive. If you are aware of what they can receive, you do not have to cut off the parts of you they cannot receive. Speak only the words that they can receive, and then you will be in control. Are you willing to create a new YOU every day? How many definitions of you have you created that are actually creating the limitation of you? Everything that is times a godzillion will you destroy and uncreate it all? ***Right and wrong, good and bad, pod and poc, all 9, shorts, boys and beyonds®.***

Whose lies and what lies and how many lies are you using to create you based on all the definitions of your name are you choosing? *Right and wrong, good and bad, pod and poc, all 9, shorts, boys and beyonds*®.

Everywhere you have misidentified and misapplied you as your name and your name as you can you now destroy and uncreate it? *Right and wrong, good and bad, pod and poc, all 9, shorts, boys and beyonds*®.

All the oaths, vows, commealties, fealties, commitments, binding and bonding contracts you have to be your name and only your name for all eternity, can you now revoke, recant, rescind, reclaim, renounce, denounce, destroy and uncreate it all? *Right and wrong, good and bad, pod and poc, all 9, shorts, boys and beyonds*®.

Are you willing to destroy all these identities you have created? *Right and wrong, good and bad, all 9, POD, POC, shorts, boys and beyonds*®.

How many jails are you using as the dominance of e=mc square as the justification of your identity are you choosing? *Right and wrong, good and bad, all 9, POD, POC, shorts, boys and beyonds*®.

Are you willing to change your style with what is required of you? Are you willing to be so irrational that no one can use one word to define you! What if you being irrational, being unpredictable is your style? It doesn't have to be but what if it was? Being beautiful and stunning and good looking does not have to be a particular suit or a silhouette. What if your stunning is your uniqueness? Your unique choice and taste? Laying the table with the beautiful silverware could be your style. Going for a picnic and carrying a picnic basket with paper plates could be your style too.

Style is not something that you look for outside of you! It is what you be, your energy is your style! Which changes every second ;)

Chapter 3

On Embracing The Moment

"DON'T SPEND TIME BEATING ON A WALL
HOPING TO TRANSFORM IT
INTO A DOOR."

Coco Chanel

How many times do we all try to transform a wall into a door even though the door is right in front of us but it's not the way we've decided it should look! What is required in that moment? Are you willing to change your point of view to receive what you would like to receive or would you like to be stuck to your points of view that only limit your receiving and capacities of being and doing what you know is possible?

Are you willing to be so irrational in every moment that the universe is seduced to provide everything you require with total ease? Everything that doesn't allow that, will you destroy and uncreate it all? ***Right and wrong, good and bad, all 9, POD, POC, shorts, boys and beyonds***®.

When you are being rational, you are trying to understand whatever is going on and put sense to every movement. Has head tripping ever created greater for you? Not for me! Being rational requires judgment, requires a whole lot of rules and that my friends is a zone with no play and limited possibility.

What if being in 10 second increments is your greatest gift? You don't have to be fickle minded when you are choosing every 10 seconds, you are just being the energy of what is required in the moment, you are embracing the moment. We stop ourselves from creating greater all the time by trying to be rational, trying to be like everyone else, trying to follow the "norm". Let's stop doing that, shall we? Let's stop letting other people's judgments affect us, affect our choices for it is not their journey. It is yours and your knowing. How many times did you know it's time to change something but you didn't because of what people would say, because your business clients would get offended and eventually it never worked out. Why? Because you knew it was time to change something but you let other people's judgments and expectations cloud your knowing.

How many jails are you using as the dominance of e=mc square as the justification of being rational are you choosing? ***Right and wrong, good and bad, all 9, POD, POC, shorts, boys and beyonds®.***

How many jails are you using as the dominance of e=mc square as the justification of fear of change are you choosing? ***Right and wrong, good and bad, all 9, POD, POC, shorts, boys and beyonds®.***

Whose lies, what lies and how many faux beingnesses are you using to create the constant you are choosing?

Right and wrong, good and bad, all 9, POD, POC, shorts, boys and beyonds®.

How much change are you willing to receive and have? ***Right and wrong, good and bad, all 9, POD, POC, shorts, boys and beyonds®.***

You don't have to keep choosing the same things my friends! Your past does not have to be your future! Do you know how? By choosing something different in the present.

Are you willing to ask, "What is required of me in this moment?" "What can I do right now that I couldn't do yesterday?"

"What molecules can I shift to create a different future?"

"What am I unwilling to be that if I would be it would actualize this with total ease?"

The past does not define you! The present does not define you and the future most definitely does not define you. How many times have we heard the saying "Your choices define you"? Friends, your choices do not define you. A choice is a choice made in those 10 seconds. If it creates greater, awesome. It does not mean that the same choice will create greater in the future too! On the other hand, if a choice doesn't create greater, please do not go into judgment of you, your choice and your creation. It was just a choice guys, you can choose different next time but if you solidify your judgment about how wrong your choice is/was and make it a reality it becomes a massive limitation to creating a greater future.

Your points of view create your reality! If your point of view is this choice is BAD! Even if it creates greater for you, for your world, you wont choose it because you are clouded with the judgment that it's BAD! Guys, there is nothing known as good and bad, right and wrong. If something has created greater for someone people have termed it as "Good" and decided that that is good for everyone and same goes for bad, right and wrong!

Just because it worked for person x does not mean it'll work for you and just because it created a "disaster" for someone else does not mean it won't create happiness for you! Just choose! If you know something will create happiness for you and the thought of choosing it lights up your world and expands your being and creates more space in your world, just choose it! Don't go into judgments, expectations, projections, rejections, separations. Choose and let the universe show you. And did you forget that the power tool of question is always by your side. Every second from choosing it to actualizing it you can ask a question. Just because it's light in the moment of choice does not mean you have to solidify it! Ask a question. Each second provides a new possibility. What if the creation of something magnificent started with choosing something, not for the outcome of it but just so you can choose something different?

For example, if there's a girl who has a huge judgment of being in a relationship, she chooses to go on a date with someone. It does not mean she has to get into a committed relationship with him just because she went for dinner and the intention of setting them up was for a relationship. What if her choosing to explore opened up a huge possibility of someone contributive to show up? She doesn't have to continue meeting the guy if she doesn't like him or if they don't get along but what if he introduces her to a friend of his who matches the energy of her ask?

If she hadn't chosen a different possibility of even exploring, she might never have opened the doors to someone else, even though she was asking.

Don't be vested in the outcome of how things will show up. Be willing to explore the moment, enjoy the moment, be present in the moment and be willing to explore possibilities every 10 seconds as anything that becomes solid, becomes a judgment not a possibility, even if it started off as an awareness and a possibility!

How many points of view are you using to spin awarenesses and possibilities into judgments are you choosing? Everything that is will you destroy and un-create it all? *Right and wrong, good and bad, all 9, POD, POC, shorts, boys and beyonds*®.

How many JAILS are you using to create the dominance of E=mc2 as the creation of your future from fixed points of view, fixed realities, fixed beingnesses, fixed thoughts, feelings and emotions and fixed lies that keeps you from creating beyond the limitations you've defined as you? ***Right and wrong, good and bad, all 9, POD, POC, shorts, boys and beyonds®.***

All of your past experience, everything you've created in the past 6 months that you've decided defines the next 6 months can you destroy and uncreate that? ***Right and wrong, good and bad, all 9, POD, POC, shorts, boys and beyonds®.***

I was on a call with the very beautiful Julia Sotas when she spoke about spurning. According to google, spurning is to reject someone with contempt or disdain.

How much do we all spurn ourselves, reject ourselves just so we can carry forward the decision we made years back or a while ago as though that proves a rightness? Everything that is can you destroy and uncreate that please? ***Right and wrong, good and bad, all 9, POD, POC, shorts, boys and beyonds®.***

What if spurning yourself for all the decisions you've made was the greatest unkindness you've done? Are you willing to change that?

We also tend to spurn ourselves a lot in moments when we make ourselves wrong for a choice that we made in the past and swear never to go down that road ever again. We reject with complete contempt in those moments as well.

What jails are you using to create the dominance of e=mc2 as only spurning others to have and maintain the rightness of you and your choices are you choosing? ***Right and wrong, good and bad, pod and poc, all 9, shorts, boys and beyonds*** What jails are you using to create the dominance of e=mc2 as only spurning yourself to have and maintain the rightness of you and your choices are you choosing? ***Right and wrong, good and bad, pod and poc, all 9, shorts, boys and beyonds***

Chapter 4

On Power

"A STRONG WOMAN LOOKS A CHALLENGE IN THE EYE AND GIVES IT A WINK."

Gina Carey

People have this idea that power means being unkind, selfish and cutting off caring. Caring about you is recognizing you ARE the power. Caring for you is being willing to totally receive. You cannot have your reality if you do not care for you.

Power is not sitting on top of each other, power is not controlling. True power is being in interesting point of view, having no judgment of what shows up, how it shows up, but being willing to ask another question.

When you are willing to ask another question, you know you have the power to change anything. When you are in interesting point of view, you are in control since you wont resist or react and wont align and agree. Something can have control and power over you only if you have a charge attached to it, if you are in allowance (interesting point of view) of it, it has no effect on you.

Power is energy, unlimited. Expansive, growing, magnificent, glorious, fabulous, exuberant and quick energy. It is everywhere. There is no diminishment of self in power and there is no diminishment of another. When you are being power, you are being in totality-self! And when you are self, you are being energy, and as energy, all is connected to you, which means unlimited supplies of money are connected as well.

Have you noticed how when people say I'm claiming my power back they never do? It's because they should be claiming their potency. People are not powerless, they are impotent. People like believing they don't have any power and that they are powerless. It's a lie. So everywhere you have misidentified and misapplied power as not the potency it is and everything you've done to call yourself powerless when what you are really doing is creating impotence. Revoke, recant, rescind, reclaim, renounce, denounce, destroy and uncreate all

of this? ***Right and wrong, good and bad, pod, poc, all
9, shorts, boys, and beyonds®.***

If you claim your potency, how would that be different from power? It's not force, it's substantial energy
availability, not a force you use against or to overcome.
Power is always about overcoming an obstacle, which
means you have already judged and decided you have
an obstacle to overcome. So claim your potency, not
your power. As the potency of you, you have every energy available to work with.

Potency is the ability to be the energies of change and
transformation. If you are willing to be that which is the
catalyst for change, then everything will change around
you. When you are not, then you are the effect of everything.

The potency of your life is the willingness to have
everything come with ease. The unwillingness to receive
in any area of your life creates the dis- ease.

When you are impotent, you open yourself to diffi-
culties, tragedies, and problems. When you are willing
to be potent, this does not occur.

The real power in life is about being potent enough
to change anything. It is not power you are looking for,
but potency. Power here on planet earth is about what?

"I've got a bigger gun than you, I have a bigger dick than you do, I have bigger tits than you do; therefore, I am more powerful than you are." Potency is the ability to change or transform anything, instantaneously, at will by your very character of being alone.

If you were truly the potency of you, you would be competent at everything. Then you would have no excuse for not having any money.

If you were present all the time, you would be potent all the time, because you would perceive, know, be, and receive everything. Being totally present all the time does not require more effort than being unconscious. Checking out means you miss every opportunity that is being given to you by the universe.

As you become more you, nobody will see you. Nobody will notice. Make everything you do and say infinite – bigger than the universe. You'll get away with everything. People never see true potency. It's outside of their reality. So, you know what'll happen if you look for validation! ;) Others not acknowledging your potency has nothing to do with you and your phenomenance, it's just that people cannot recognize it in this reality.

In any area in your life where you feel powerless or impotent, you can run this process on yourself continuously:

What potency are you refusing with the impotence you are choosing? Everything that is will you, revoke, recant, rescind, reclaim, renounce, denounce, destroy and uncreate all of this? ***Right, Wrong, Good, Bad, POD, POC, All 9, shorts, boys, and beyonds®.***

What being are you avoiding with the impotence you are choosing? Everything that is will you, revoke, recant, rescind, reclaim, renounce, denounce, destroy and uncreate all of this? ***Right, Wrong, Good, Bad, POD, POC, All 9, shorts, boys, and beyonds®.***

What bastardization of infinite power and potency are you using to create the pathetic pile of shit life you are choosing? Everything that is times a godzillion will you destroy and uncreate it all? ***Right and wrong, good and bad, pod and poc, all 9, shorts, boys and beyonds®.***

Most people think their anger is their power. People suppress their anger to prove that they're not powerful, so they can prove that they are a victim to everybody else. You perceive that they could kill you in a heartbeat, but they are suppressing their anger and acting as if they wouldn't hurt a fly, so you end up thinking you're nuts.

People's suppressed anger comes at you in strange ways that you don't know what to do with. You go, "What do I do with this?" but that's not really a question, because you have already decided that this is something you can't handle, because they won't handle it or change it. So, "What choice do I really have here? I can kill them, I can get stronger than them, or I can make them suppress and repress themselves more, and control them through that." But that's not usually the one you choose. Most of you try to suck that energy out of them so they'll get better. Or you try to get more powerful than them, but that's not real power; that's domination. There is a real power – caring. When you have somebody who does anger, if you do more caring than they can do anger, they melt.

Humanoid women want to go out and conquer the world, but many of them stayed home and had babies. There was a really oppressive time for humanoid women, which was the basis of the women's movement. But unfortunately, movements go too far one way or the other. It's really not about man or woman; it's about human or humanoid. If they had made it about human and humanoid and the difference between the two, it would have been a different world. But they didn't do that; they made it about man and woman. They created opposition of the sexes, which really does not help at all.

The point of view that men have suppressed women all these years is a lie. No. Humans have suppressed humanoids. That's the thing that nobody is willing to look at and that's the lie that keeps this other insanity in existence. In the world, there have been women who were always out there, owning property and doing things they weren't supposed to be able to do. Why? Nothing was going to stop them. But women have gotten to the place where they do explosion of anger, rage, fury, and hate in order to get over the suppression that they have misidentified and misapplied belongs to men, rather than humans. Humans suppress humanoids. Everything has been done to suppress humanoids, to put them down, make them less. Humanoids are always wrong. You don't fit, no matter what. If you're a humanoid, you're not going to fit anywhere. The human perspective is, "You have to fit into my reality."

Human women will do more to put a humanoid woman down than men will ever do. They will do everything in their power to tell you that you are wrong.

Human women will tell you all the time that you need to stay home, have babies, and have a man take care of you, instead of going out searching for answers. But humanoid women would rather die than stay home and shop. They can't help themselves. They have to find a way to create some kind of wave of change in the world. Humanoid women will always find a way of creating something different.

Procrastination is a huge example of power. We put off so much till the last minute as a way to prove our power that we are capable of achieving the task at such a quick pace.

What energy, space and consciousness can I be to allow me to be the power I truly be and never put anything off for all eternity?

Would an infinite being ever require to prove anything? No! An infinite being just is, an infinite being just knows and perceives his/her greatness. Proving requires you to believe first that you are not that and then go into resistance in order to believe that you are being that. Are you? No, you are resisting.

So, everything you have done to buy proving as your point of view, can you destroy and uncreate it please? *Right and wrong, good and bad, pod and poc, all 9, shorts, boys and beyonds®.*

Are you willing to pull the energy of true power into your life? Okay, Let's pull it in.

Style your Life

Energy Pull

Get comfortable, you can keep sitting, lying down or whatever else you are doing. Now, get present with the energy and the definition that you've given to power. Look at it, look at every molecule, perceive the energy of it. Now, everything that you've defined power as, can you destroy and uncreate it please? ***Right and wrong, good and bad, pod and poc, all 9, shorts, boys and beyonds**®*. Ask, is this energy creating greater? Would inviting the energy of true power change and shift something? Are you willing to have that? Everything that doesn't allow that will you destroy and uncreate it? ***Right and wrong, good and bad, pod and poc, all 9, shorts, boys and beyonds**®*. Ask for the energy of true power to show up. Kindness is power, caring is power, being in interesting point of view is power. Now put that energy in front of you, pull energy from the universe into that into your body and out of your body. Keep pulling tsunamis of energy through the universe, through the energy, into your body and out of your body. And now ask "What will it take for me to be power?"

Every morning and every night say "I be power/I am power" as many times as you may like. Invite it into your world. What else is possible®?

Chapter 5

On Beauty

"I THINK THERE IS BEAUTY IN EVERYTHING.
WHAT 'NORMAL' PEOPLE PERCEIVE AS UGLY,
I CAN USUALLY SEE SOMETHING OF BEAUTY
IN IT."

Alexander McQueen

Before we begin talking about beauty, all the definitions, judgments, separations, rejections, conclusions
you have about beauty can you destroy and uncreate
that please? ***Right and wrong, good and bad, pod and
poc, all 9, shorts, boys and beyonds®.***

Whose lies, what lies and how many faux beingnesses
are you using to create the beautiful you are choosing?

***Right and wrong, good and bad, pod and poc, all 9, shorts, boys and beyonds*®.**

Are you willing to let go of the lies you bought from others as to what beauty is and let that which is true for you to show up? Everything that doesn't allow that can you destroy and uncreate it? ***Right and wrong, good and bad, pod and poc, all 9, shorts, boys and beyonds*®.**

What is beauty? There are thousands of definitions of what beauty is and how it should show up. For some, beauty is sadness, for some beauty is pain, for some beauty is a smile, for some beauty lies in the eyes of the beholder. Beauty can be to be free and act naturally, according to what is true for you! To be able to just sit and laugh with someone is so difficult nowadays. It's because of the barriers that we have so high as though that's what is required to protect us. It's a lie. Having a barrier is like being Rapunzel in that tall castle with a tiny window to peek through. Is that how you would like to be or would you rather be willing to receive all that this beautiful universe has to gift? Let's do an exercise, shall we? Okay right now close your eyes and perceive how high your walls/barriers are, ask for the barriers to go down. All you have to do is ask. "Barriers down". Be present with it. If you like you can push your barriers down with your hands. Get a sense of how high they are and now place your hands there and gently push them down and throw it into the earth. The earth does not have a point of view of anything, for it everything is just energy.

And after your barriers go down, it is so much ease to just be, to smile, to laugh.

Have you heard of the saying beauty begins when you start to be you? I kind of agree. I would just say you have always been beautiful, when you start embracing you more, you get to see the beauty of you! My dear, you are already so beautiful. You are not willing to see the beauty of you, because if you did, you would have to see the beauty in the world. You would have to change your point of view from judgment to aesthetics.

Every time you look at someone and judge yourself can you ask "What's right about me I'm not getting?". Every time you look at something and judge it, say "Interesting point of view I have this point of view".

What have you invented as beauty? Everything that is will you destroy and uncreate it all? ***Right and wrong, good and bad, POC, POD, all 9, shorts, boys, and beyonds®.***

What have you invented as not beauty? Everything that is will you destroy and uncreate it all? ***Right and***

***wrong, good and bad, POC, POD, all 9, shorts, boys, and beyonds**.

We are used to judging a book by its cover, it's usually not our wisest choice but people have placed a huge weight on "first impressions". That my friends, is done from sheer judgment. Judgment is not only the ones we don't like hearing. Judgment is anything that has an energy attached to it. A judgment can be positive, a judgment can be negative according to what we are willing to hear and receive but as long as it has a charge, a significance attached to it, it is judgment. Looking at a man who's an asshole for being an asshole is not a judgment, it's just an acknowledgment of who he is. Similarly, looking at someone and deciding he/she is the most stunning person is judgment. Most stunning according to whom? According to whose definitions? What you see as stunning could be outrageous for someone else. If you look at a person and appreciate him/her as just being in a different space to you, it changes the energy because anything (even if it's "positive") that has an energy and a charge to it is a judgment.

How many of you have decided that beauty is a luxury? How many of you when you find something beautiful and inviting, instead of going towards it run away from it? Are you even willing to have it in your life? What if beauty was in the little moments too? What if beauty didn't have to be luxury? Anything that makes your being expand is beauty my friends. Why would you keep yourself from that?

Everywhere you bought into the lie that beauty is expensive can you destroy and uncreate that? ***Right and wrong, good and bad, POC, POD, all 9, shorts, boys, and beyonds®.***

Choose beauty my friends, for you are what defines it. You are it, be it.

For me, a beautiful world is a world of no judgment. A space to choose whatever you would like to choose without having to judge yourself over and over again. Are you willing to invite that into your life? Are you willing to expand on the beauty that already exists in your world? And everything that doesn't allow you to know, be and perceive that will you destroy and uncreate it all? ***Right and wrong, good and bad, POC, POD, all 9, shorts, boys, and beyonds®.***

Being willing to receive is beautiful, it is also the energy of being a lady. A lady is someone who is willing to receive everything, the compliments, the judgments, the hatred, the love and doesn't stop being herself just because all those are projected at her. Being willing to receive everything is willing to be in interesting point of view. When others judge you and are unwilling to receive you, recognize that it is something they see in you that they judge themselves for which has them rejecting and resisting you. It's a choice they are making, what if you continue being you, without judging them? This would give them the freedom of choice as well. The freedom to choose to receive.

A lady doesn't change who or what she is based on how much money she receives or how much money she makes. A lady continues to be a lady irrespective of how rich or "poor" she is.

Everywhere you've decided you will only be a lady when you reach a certain peak of wealth, will you destroy and uncreate it all? ***Right and wrong, good and bad, POC, POD, all 9, shorts, boys, and beyonds®.***

What have you defined as being a lady that keeps you rejecting the lady you truly be? ***Right and wrong, good and bad, POC, POD, all 9, shorts, boys, and beyonds®.***

What if you already are being a lady and just haven't acknowledged it because its always been? Everything that is, will you destroy and uncreate it all? ***Right and wrong, good and bad, POC, POD, all 9, shorts, boys, and beyonds®.***

What if the beauty of elegance is in being in no point of view, not resisting and not reacting? How much of that are you already being?

My beautiful friends, you are truly beautiful. Are you finally willing to embrace your beauty?

Chapter 6

On Bodies

**"A GIRL SHOULD BE TWO THINGS:
WHO AND WHAT SHE WANTS."**

Coco Chanel

Think of having a friend and never talking to him/her never acknowledging him/her, never saying "Hey!" Your body is an extremely conscious being. It has a consciousness of its own. Why do we have bodies? Like Dr. Dain said, so you can feel the sun on your skin, so you can climb a tree, so you can feel the water when you step into the ocean.

Our bodies have capacities and capabilities way beyond what has ever been told to us. Well, talking about being told, we're only told how wrong our bodies are, how we should separate from it, how we should keep it covered, how it invites people to us so we must cut off ourselves from it.

Everything you've done to buy into the point of view that your body is wrong and it must be separated, can you destroy and uncreate it all? ***Right and wrong, good and bad, POC, POD, all 9, shorts, boys, and beyonds®.***

Your body is a creation of your points of views! When you look at yourself in the mirror, you're not looking at yourself, you're looking at all the judgments you have of your body which your body has now shifted and changed to become that! What if we could start looking at our bodies from the eyes of someone who doesn't judge us? How much can that change? What if you could look at your body from the eyes of infinite being your are instead of the judgments of finiteness?

We end up following what others have told us about bodies, what the religious point of view is, what the spiritual point of view is. My friends, I ask you what is your point of view? Not what you heard from your mother, not what you learned from your friends, what is YOURS?

Style your Life

Did you get an answer, most likely not. Why? Well because no one has ever asked you that before and because you have none! You have no point of view about your body. You picked it up from others. How does that work? Well, it's like if X has a judgment of Y being shy, too soft, boring, indecisive and if Y agrees and aligns with it or resists and reacts to it, it will stick to her world and exist in her world (instead if she would have been in interesting point of view, it would have just passed through her and not stuck to her). So when Y goes out for a meeting with A, A will hear "soft", "indecisive" and if she doesn't have the tool "who does this belong to?", she'll most likely think she's soft, she's indecisive and your points of view are what create your body, her body will show up based on those points of view being impelled on her which to start with weren't even hers! Do you see how this works?

It's quite simple really, "Who does this belong to?" and "interesting point of view I/you have this point of view" works like magic. If you give yourself that space of realizing that your body as of now might not even be based on your creation. Well, technically it is your creation since you agreed and aligned/ resisted and reacted but it's not your creation to carry out someone else's reality. Cute, not smart ;)

Don't worry, I've done it too. ;)

This is what it's usually like when you let something stick to your world, that others pick up on and make it theirs and the cycle carries on.

What religious and spiritual point of view are you using to create your body are you choosing? *Right and wrong, good and bad, POC, POD, all 9, shorts, boys, and beyonds*.

How many jails (judgments, agendas, inventions and lies) are you using to create the domination of $E=mc2$ (Evil, mediocrity and corruption) as always trying to use your rational mind and your rational conclusions rather than your irrational awareness that keeps you from the joy of having, being, doing creating and generating your body beyond your wildest dreams. ***Right and wrong, good and bad, POC, POD, all 9, shorts, boys, and beyonds®.***

How many jails are you using to create the dominance of E=mc2 as the creation of sexualness from fixed points of view, fixed realities, fixed beingnesses, fixed thoughts, feelings and emotions, and fixed lies that keeps you from creating beyond the limitations you've defined as real that are not? ***Right and wrong, good and bad, POC, POD, all 9, shorts, boys, and beyonds®.***

What jails are you using to create the dominance of e=mc square as the fixed points of view, fixed lies, fixed realities, feelings and emotions, form, structure and significance, fixed beingnesses for making you wrong in totality with and for having physical reality? ***Right and wrong, good and bad, POC, POD, all 9, shorts, boys, and beyonds®.***

If your body got the future that it desired, how much greater would it be than the future you've decided? Everything you've done to invalidate all of that, will you destroy and uncreate it? ***Right and wrong, good and bad, POC, POD, all 9, shorts, boys, and beyonds®.***

Whose lies and what lies are you using to avoid the awareness of your body's desires are you choosing? ***Right and wrong, good and bad, POC, POD, all 9, shorts, boys, and beyonds®.***

How many jails are you using to create the dominance of E=mc2 as the justification of creation of your body as a limitation are you choosing? ***Right and wrong, good and bad, POC, POD, all 9, shorts, boys, and beyonds®.***

We tend to create our bodies based on the projections that were thrown at us as a child. We buy it as real and keep projecting that on our bodies as though that is what is us. No, it is what we use to reject our bodies. What if you knew your body has a kindness for you, a gentleness with you and a generosity with you, what would be truly possible? We are energetic beings and our bodies are energetic bodies but nobody ever told us that, nobody ever told them either. They don't understand it. They're doing the best they can. Your body has capabilities and capacities way beyond what you have decided are real and true.

Whose lies, what lies and how many lies are you using that keeps you from being the phenomenance of conscious embodiment of you, you are choosing?

Right and wrong, good and bad, POD, POC, all 9, shorts, boys, and beyonds®.

Whose lies, what lies and how many lies are you using that has you creating the finiteness of embodiment you are choosing? ***Right and wrong, good and bad, POD, POC, all 9, shorts, boys, and beyonds®.***

Whose lies, what lies and how many lies are you using that keeps you from accessing and embodying all energies? ***Right and wrong, good and bad, POD, POC, all 9, shorts, boys, and beyonds®.***

How many jails are you using as the dominance of e=mc square as the justification of embodiment of this reality are you choosing? ***Right and wrong, good and bad, pod and poc, all 9, shorts, boys and beyonds®.***

What have you made so vital, valuable and real about human mechanistic embodiment that keeps you from the joyful, playful, creative, expansive ease of humanoid embodiment that you and your body are here to create and be? ***Right and wrong, good and bad, pod and poc, all 9, shorts, boys and beyonds®.*** When you look in the mirror and judge your body, your body creates more of the judgment you have of it. Instead: ***"Thank you body for putting up with me."*** When you think you're hungry, ask your body if it would like to eat or drink. Your body likes to be spacey and spacious, which is actually what happens when you're hungry. We try to take that away by filling ourselves up with food. Food should actually be a homeopathic to release our body's energy. It takes 96% of the energy in the calories in food to digest it. The purpose of food is to kill your body.

Animals will eat what they need. We eat what we **like. We think we get energy from food, which is a** lie. We defend against our bodies. We don't listen to them.

What stupidity are you using to create the food that will kill your body you are choosing? Everything that is times a godzillion will you destroy and uncreate it all? *Right and wrong, good and bad, pod and poc, all 9, shorts, boys and beyonds®.*

What emotions am I using to create the body I am choosing? *Right and wrong, good and bad, pod and poc, all 9, shorts, boys and beyonds®.*

How much judgment are you using to make sure your body cannot receive the joy of the food and drink you are choosing? *Right and wrong, good and bad, pod and poc, all 9, shorts, boys and beyonds®.*

Whose dietary scale of insanity are you eating from? *Right and wrong, good and bad, pod and poc, all 9, shorts, boys and beyonds*®.

Also, if you are willing to be in interesting point of view with your body, in a space of no judgment your body will show up far greater than you ever thought it could be. Your body is so beautiful! Are you going to give it the space to show up as it would like to?

As you start to talk to your body and be a space of no judgment with it, it will shed tons of weight as well. A lot of times, we hold onto weight as a way of hiding, we end up storing all the judgments in our body when we resist it or agree with it. Are you ready to change all of that now?

Body Types

Pear shaped, hour glass, rectangle, lean, inverted triangle, do those really exist?

Okay, so let me ask you a question have there been days your body was an "hourglass" and the next day it became "pearshaped"? Have there been moments when your waist was so slim and the next morning it wasn't? It's happened hasn't it? So, how can you be one particular body type? Your body has capacities and capabilities of changing and shifting all the time. Asking it and labelling it as a certain type is really not wise. Your body will change shapes, and sizes. Now, I know you would like your body to be a certain type wouldn't you? There's an exercise for you on the next page. Look at each body type, each one of them is different. For 5 days, ask your body what it would like to look like. You, your mind might not want to look like it at all, ask your body. It may be one of these, or it may not be one of these. Do the muscle testing. Stand up and ask your body to show you "yes". You just have to ask "Body give me a yes" and your body will move either front, back, left or right. Then ask "Body give me a No" and your body will show you what a no is for it. Then you can hold a piece of garment in your hands and ask your body the questions "Body, do you like wearing this? Would you like to wear this hereon?". Your body will talk to you. Are you willing to listen? If you happen not to get a clear awareness, it could be because of your mind interfering in between. So, say "Everything is the opposite of what it appears to be and nothing is the opposite of what it appears to be", this will stop your mind from interfering and then you'll pick up on your awareness instantly.

And now ask "Body would you like to look like this?", go through each body type and ask every day for

5 days and see if your body wants to look the same or if you get different ones every day.

Day 1

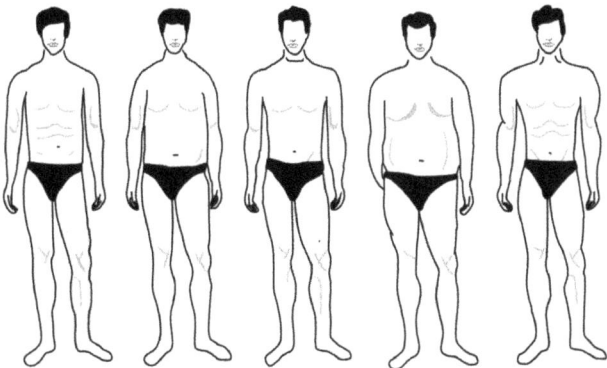

Day 2

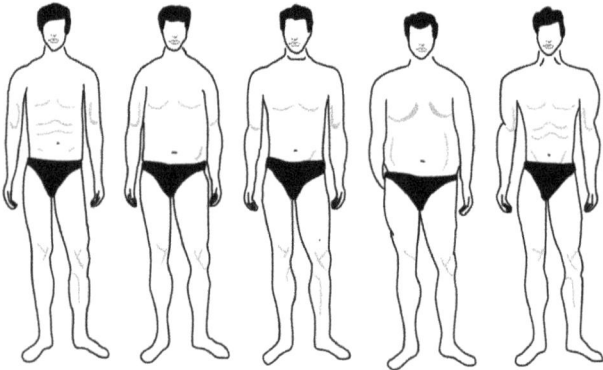

Day 3

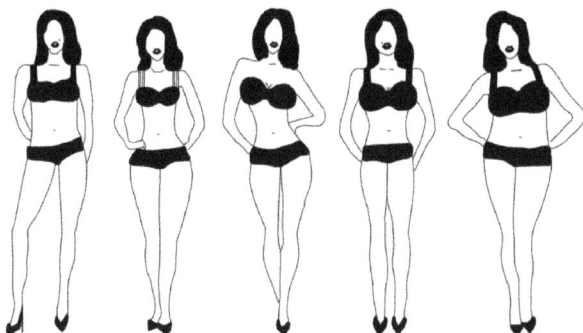

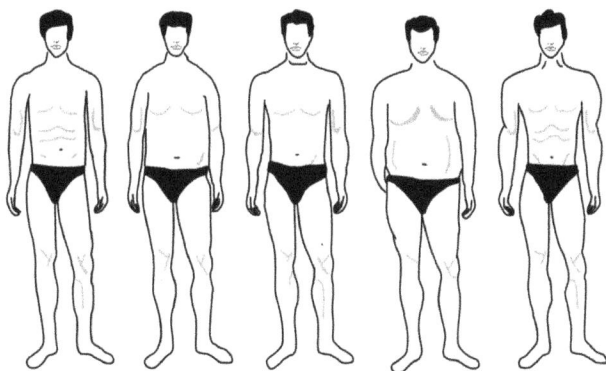

Day 4

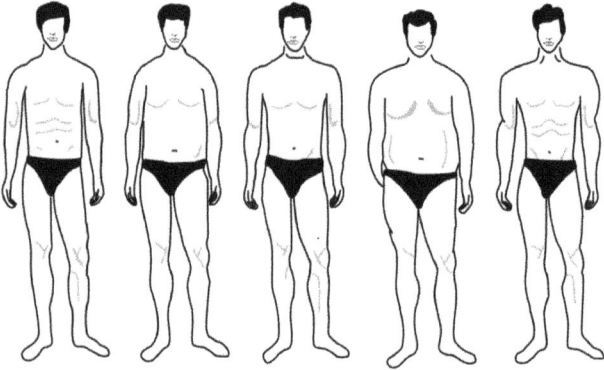

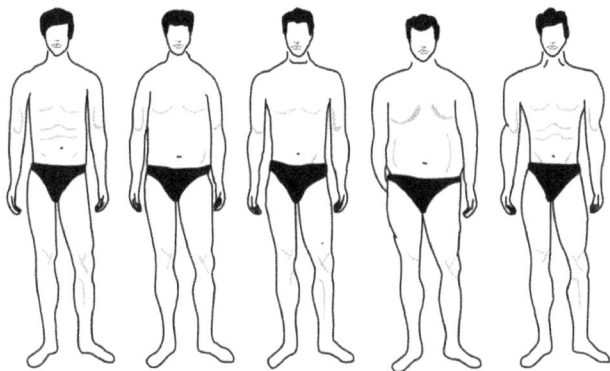

Day 5

Now that day 5 is over, look at all of them and ask your body if there's an attribute of each of them it likes, would it want something from one, something from another one. If it does, you can ask it to show up as that. You can do this with anything. Just ask your body if it would like to show up as that and then talk to your body and ask it to actualize. When it shows up, it'll be according to what your body perceives it as and will be great because your body will enjoy looking like it.

Let the significance of body shapes and types go, your body is really capable of way more if you allow it.

Everything you've done to justify all the body shapes as reality can you destroy and uncreate that? ***Right and wrong, good and bad, POC, POD, all 9, shorts, boys, and beyonds®.***

Your body has capacities to change and shift every-day. What if your knowing that could have you creating a body that you desire?

Do the muscle testing with food every day for 5 days and see how your body changes. With everything you eat, every single bite you take, ask your body "Body do you want to ingest this?", if you get a yes go ahead but don't eat to oblivion, the second food starts to taste like rubber or cardboard, stop eating. It could be after 8 bites. If you're willing to hear and listen to your body, your body will show you the capacities it has that you never knew were possible.

Chapter 7

Your Wardrobe Workout

"JUST LET THE WARDROBE DO THE ACTING."

Jack Nicholson

What if you could use your clothes to deliver what the next person can receive? If you're going for an interview, ask the clothes, talk to the clothes. Tap into the energy of the interview and ask "What energy, space and consciousness can my body and I be to be received with total ease?" and then ask "What can I wear that would match the energy of what the interviewer is looking for with total ease?". You can ask the clothes to talk to the interviewer too, ask it to speak and communicate your brilliance to him/her. Let it be your voice as well.

Each piece of cloth, each pair of sandals have their own energy. Just the way our energies shift every 10 seconds, what I/our body would or can receive from the energy of that garment shifts every 10 seconds. Have you noticed how you can wear the exact same outfit twice but your vibe, your look can be completely different. On one occasion if something is making you look elegant, it can make you look funky too when worn at a different time. Why? Yes, the way you do your hair could be different but it is also the energy of your body that has shifted and what it would like to receive from the outfit. My point of view is that the energy of an outfit is just energy, it's not a defined energy. What is elegant for one person can be totally vulgar for someone else. It really is what energy your body picks up from the outfit, it could be the perceptions, expectations, conclusions and judgments you are picking up of all the people involved in creating that outfit. Your body knows, it is extremely aware.

Let's do a quick exercise on styling yourself-

Get present with your body, put your feet on the ground and feel connected to the earth. Now, let's ask the body what it would like to wear, shall we? Remember your body has its consciousness. Do we dress for our being or our body? Our body right? So, lets ask our body!

Your hair- Connect to the molecules of your hair and ask it what it would like to look like today? Go with that!

Your outfit- Look at your wardrobe and ask your body to show you what it would like to wear. You can even use muscle testing to ask your body if there's a particular colour it would like on that day, a particular silhouette. If your body gives you a yes then go ahead with that and know your body will feel extremely nurtured, cared for and whichever energy it is asking to be that day.

Your footwear- Ask your feet what it would like to wear.

Accessories- What is the energy of you today? What is it that you are dressing for? Does it require accessories? For me personally, I always love accessorizing myself. It's like adding a special touch. A beautiful pair of pearl earrings in my view always do the magic if it's a casual look you are desiring. Always ask the outfit what it would like to get accessorized with. It will give you all the answers you require.

Your Workout

Could having clutter around you also lead to cluttered thoughts? If you clear the clutter around you, in your space, would it be possible that your being would be more expansive and your body happier? Clearing clutter on the outside also helps in clearing the unwanted energy from your life, clearing clutter from within. Are you ready to start?

Let's start with your wardrobe.

Open your wardrobe and take every single thing out. Look at each and every outfit, accessory, footwear just see it all. Clutter does not allow space, clutter keeps you from creation. Now, lets start the detox and clear the clutter shall we?

Don't get overwhelmed, it's a lie- an infinite being can never get overwhelmed. This is going to be exciting. Start with your tops, shirts, basically everything waist up. You are going to connect with every piece before you choose what to do with it. Hold the outfit in your hands and ask your body questions "Body, do you like wearing this? Would you like to wear this hereon?" Hear what you get. You can do muscle testing too. Stand up and ask your body to show you "yes". You just have to ask "Body give me a yes" and your body will move either front, back, left or right. Then ask "Body give me a No" and your body will show you what a no is for it. Then you can hold a piece of garment in your hands and ask your body the questions "Body, do you like wearing this? Would you like to wear this hereon?". Your body will talk to you. Are you willing to listen? If you happen not to get a clear awareness, it could be because of your mind interfering in between. So, say "Everything is the opposite of what it appears to be and nothing is the opposite of what it appears to be", this will stop your mind from interfering and then you'll pick up on your awareness instantly.

You can also talk to the garment and ask it "If I keep you will you make me money?". Now for some of them, your body might not enjoy wearing it but if it's going to make you money, well I would still keep it.

Do this with every single thing lying in your wardrobe and you can go through the colour chart in the next chapter to create combinations too. Have fun with this, spend 40 seconds with each garment and see the shift in your wardrobe. You'll love playing with it. While putting the clothes up again, you can ask the clothes to show you where they want to be kept. It's going to be fun, are you willing to explore it? Might be too much fun, don't do it, you might get too much information and it might expand your world way too much. ;)

Use the same tools to clear your room, your house, your workspace.

How much chaos can you instill in the order of clutter?

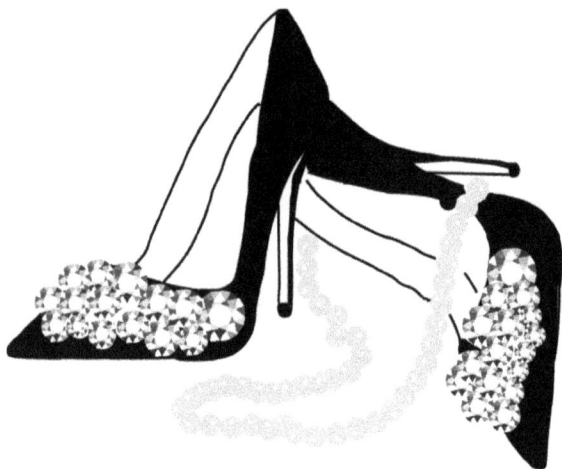

On Wealth

"STYLE IS WEARING AN EVENING DRESS TO MCDONALD'S, WEARING HEELS TO PLAY FOOTBALL. IT IS PERSONALITY, CONFIDENCE AND SEDUCTION."

John Galliano

Do you have that one favourite outfit of yours that you know you'll always have a great time in, that special piece of jewellery, that lucky perfume that'll just make your day, something you put on and you just feel so happy and you tell yourself it's because of that memory behind the moment related to your outfit/jewellery etc? I'm here to burst your bubble guys! Your outfit, your perfume, that accessory isn't lucky. It's your body feeling happy and a space of no judgment with that what you put on, your being (often referred to as spirit/soul), being in a space of expansiveness. It's the knowing that someone has your back, it's the knowing that you'll be just fine. Yes, things can have your back. Everything has an energy right? I have a ring that I was gifted by my beautiful parents and sister when I graduated. I chose the design, I looked at it and knew it had to be with me. The moment I put it on my world expanded, my being recognized this, this energy, I knew my ring loved me and I knew my ring always had my back. Initially I would wear it sparingly, once in a while because I had decided that it's "too abundant" to be worn regularly. The days I would wear it, I would have an awesome time. Not that people didn't judge me or not like me but I didn't need them to like me, I would be happy being me, being with the beautiful people who actually care for me rather than those who are busy judging themselves under the pretense of judging me. I casually wondered one day why I wouldn't choose to wear this beautiful ring all the time (beautiful not because it's expensive, not based on its physical appearance but beautiful because it's a space of no judgment for me). So, one day I just chose not to take it off ☺. Why should I have to invite this energy of abundance with this space of no judgment only on "special occasions", parties etc? I'll have this all the time. I'm willing to make this energy my life, my every day moment, not just a special occasion moment of abundance.

On the other hand, there are also moments when we hide our abundance or else tone it down in front of people because we wouldn't want to attract too much attention, right? Are you willing to let that all go now and just be who you be, irrespective of who is around and who is not?

So, how much have you decided you have to only have the "abundant things" on days people are there to see? Are you willing to be this energy with yourself? Everything that is will you destroy and uncreate it all? ***Right and wrong, good and bad, POC, POD, all 9, shorts, boys, and beyonds®.***

Are you willing to be honor, trust, gratitude, allowance, vulnerability with abundant living? Everything that is will you destroy and uncreate it all? ***Right and wrong, good and bad, POC, POD, all 9, shorts, boys, and beyonds®.***

How much have you decided you have to hide all the "abundant things" on days people are there to see? Are you willing to be this energy with yourself at all times? Everything that is will you destroy and uncreate it all?

Right and wrong, good and bad, POC, POD, all 9, shorts, boys, and beyonds®.

What lies, whose lies, how many lies are you using to resist and reject the abundance of you, you truly be? Everything that is will you destroy and uncreate it all? *Right and wrong, good and bad, POC, POD, all 9, shorts, boys, and beyonds®.*

Are you willing to let abundance and wealth know you would like to actually have it or are you busy living the pathetic life pretending you're working your ass off to "earn" money and have wealth one day? Is that one day going to come? Nope, when that one day arrives it'll be "today", not good enough for you. ;)

So, everything you've done to throw all your todays away in hope of your one day can you destroy and un-create that? *Right and wrong, good and bad, POC, POD, all 9, shorts, boys, and beyonds®.*

Everything you've done/ this reality has done for you to believe that money is the creative force and source that you need will you destroy and uncreate it? *Right and wrong, good and bad, POC, POD, all 9, shorts, boys, and beyonds®.*

Style your Life

If you had a future where you had no problem with money where you had every choice available, what would you choose?

Are you willing to be the voice of wealth and possibilities? It's not about what you can buy, it's about what you can be my friends. Are you willing to dress like you would when you "become" a wealthy person?

Everything you've done to buy into the lies of how much it takes to dress as a wealthy person can you destroy and uncreate that? **Right and wrong, good and bad, POC, POD, all 9, shorts, boys, and beyonds®.**

Are you dressing for success or failure? Most people dress for failure thinking that one day they will succeed and that day they will dress successfully. Nope, they are choosing failure.

Are you willing to dress to create a future? The way you dress creates a future. What future are you dressing for? It doesn't mean you have to be in high heels and go to the grocery store with smokey eye makeup! Well, you could do that too but it surely doesn't mean that you step out looking like someone who can't afford herself/himself. *You don't want to afford yourself, you want to have the luxury of being you.* What if you knew you were luxury and you already are wealth, would you still choose to treat yourself with mediocrity? You don't have to be flashy if you don't want to, you don't have to be loud if you don't want to. You want to add your element of extravaganza to your life- what you know is possible. Gary Douglas once said, "Arrogance is walking as though you know you own the world, you just haven't paid for it yet."

So, what have you decided is loud, flashy, obnoxious, arrogant, shallow? Everything that is will you destroy and uncreate it? *Right and wrong, good and bad, POC, POD, all 9, shorts, boys, and beyonds®.*

Whose lies, what lies and how many beingnesses are you using to create the sophistication, elegance and glamour you are choosing? Everything that is will you destroy and uncreate it? *Right and wrong, good and bad, POC, POD, all 9, shorts, boys, and beyonds®.*

Do you think the price of the designer suits at probably an upmarket store is the price of its cost to be tailored? Hah! Nope! Probably not even half the price. What does it take to create a wealthy piece of suit? Fabric, dying, stitching, sampling, inspection, production, final inspection. Yes, there are various stages of a garment being actualized but what makes a garment wealthy, exclusive or average are the points of view and the judgments being impelled at it during the stages from sampling to production. Even as it makes its way into the showroom, as it is picked up from the rack and put back again how many projections and judgments are impelled at it?

If the people involved in actualizing a garment actually enjoy their job and enjoy creating that particular piece, the energy of that product will be caring, nurturing, generative too amongst lots of others. An order of a particular garment may have a quantity of 500 pieces. One piece will never be the same as the other. Why? Some may call it a different lot of fabric, some may call it a different lot of dying which is true, there are different lots that create a quantity of the same piece but for me, it is the "frame of mind" the people creating it were in during the creation. Was staying late at the production unit a way of escaping their home? Would they go do a certain task as a way to take their anger out? Could it be possible that that piece of fabric/ embellishment would have been made with anger, rage, fury, and a feeling of not being good enough and when you put it on that's what you pick up on?

Everything that is will you destroy and uncreate it all? ***Right and wrong, good and bad, POC, POD, all 9, shorts, boys, and beyonds®.***

On the other hand, if an outfit was created with fun, while laughing, after being validated for the hard work and time being put in, would it be possible that that's what gets projected at the outfit?

It's crazy isn't it? Never thought of it like that. Just looked at the suit, put it on and bought it because it looked good. So, what now?

Now is a different experience of shopping.

What if every time you walked into a store and looked at an outfit that called out to you, you touched it, felt it and heard what it had to say? Is it something that would add to your life or something that would take away? And what would it add or take away? Would it add anger, hatred, self doubt or would it add laughter, happiness, success, money? Yes, you are the creator of it all but are you willing to receive the support these things have to offer you in order to succeed, make money and add laughter? Things can really support you if you are willing to receive from them.

So, everywhere we were told we are being materialistic every time we looked at something beautiful and wanted it, will you destroy and uncreate it all? ***Right and wrong, good and bad, POC, POD, all 9, shorts, boys, and beyonds®.***

All those people who made you wrong for knowing you can have whatever you want because you had no point of view of the price tag, will you destroy and un-create it all? Are you willing to stop looking at price tags through their eyes? What if you could start looking at a price tag without any point of view, the way you always knew was possible?

Everything that doesn't allow you to know, be, perceive and receive the brilliance of your point of view, can you destroy and uncreate that? ***Right and wrong, good and bad, POC, POD, all 9, shorts, boys, and beyonds®.***

Whose point of view are you doing interesting point of view from? Is it even yours? ***Right and wrong, good and bad, POC, POD, all 9, shorts, boys, and beyonds®.***

My beautiful friends, wealth and abundance is in every molecule of this universe. The only thing that separates us from it are our points of view of what we can receive and what we can't.

Here's an exercise for you guys-

Write down all the judgments you have about money. Money is bad, dirty, leads to fights etc. Go for it. Now is the time to tell money how much you hate it.

Now, write down what you are grateful to money for. Whatever it brought into your life, the experiences, the laughter, a smile, anything. Go for it!

_____

_____

_____

_____

_____

_____

_____

_____

_____

_____

What if money was your friend and what if the judgments written by you about money were about your friend? Now, look at the first list and see it, each point and ask yourself why would your friend want to stay in your life or why would someone new want to enter your life if you had these points of view about them? Are you willing to actually have a different perspective?

Look at the second list, see each point, get a sense of it.

Ask yourself now, you would give the first list more significance for what reason? It may have shown up like that in some part of your world or not but look at what it also gave you which you are grateful for. Would you rather not see that and be grateful for it and ask for megatons more? Or would you rather stay in the pathetic pile of poo of list 1? Go ahead. Choose ☺.

Money is your friend; it has no point of view. It's you who has points of view about money and about those who have money. If you were willing to give up those points of view could you begin to receive greater? Just wondering!

Be willing to dress to be judged. Are you willing to have people throw all kinds of judgments at you just based on appearance? Did you know that every time someone judges you, and you receive it, the judgments show up in your bank account as money? Well! Judgments or Money? What do you choose?

Now why in the world would you want to create money, right?

So, *everything you've done to resist the judgments thrown at you each time you choose to show up as* you, can you destroy and uncreate that? ***Right and wrong, good and bad, pod and poc, all 9, shorts, boys and beyonds®.***

Whose lies, what lies and how many lies are you using to create the necessity of, and resistance of popularity and stardom are you choosing? ***Right and wrong, good and bad, pod and poc, all 9, shorts, boys and beyonds®.***

What will it take for you to be the social butterfly you truly be? Everything that doesn't allow that, will you destroy and uncreate it all? ***Right and wrong, good and bad, pod and poc, all 9, shorts, boys and beyonds®.***

Chapter 9

On Actualizing with Energy Pulls

> "REAL FASHION CHANGE COMES FROM REAL CHANGES IN REAL LIFE. EVERYTHING ELSE IS JUST DECORATION."
>
> *Tom Ford*

What is an energy pull? You know when you're thinking of someone and they call you? You pulled their energy right then. That moment when you're getting a tug to enter a store and when you do you find that exact dress you were looking for? That's an energy pull.

Now if you can pull someone's attention, you can also pull everything you desire into your life! I've been having a complete party with energy pulls. For me, the pulls are also a way of recognizing that the universe has your back in and with all your creations. When we pull energy, it not only creates greater for us and for everyone around us but also for everyone involved with us in our creations. Are you guys ready to embark on this adventure? Wohooo lets go!

If you're thinking how to pull energy, know there's no right and wrong way of doing this, you can't screw it up! Your very being is an energy puller. You can get someone to read these out to you as you do them, if you want to keep your eyes shut, you can also do them as you read through it and you can read it and then do it with your eyes shut too. There's no right and wrong way of doing this. You can pull energy eyes open, shut, standing, sitting, lying, sleeping.

Energy Pull 1

What energy, space and consciousness can you and your body be to acknowledge your potency with total ease? *Right and wrong, good and bad, POC, POD, all 9, shorts, boys, and beyonds®.*

Pull energy from the front of you, into your body and out of your body. Let it through.

Keep pulling. If you sense any barriers, you can ask them to go down. Barriers are energetic walls we put up as a pretense of protection. They cannot protect us, they only stop our receiving. All you can say is "Barriers down".

Keep pulling as we say the clearings, as we read through this, know you are pulling energy.

What energy, space and consciousness can you and your body be to know, be, perceive, receive all of the energy pulls with total ease? ***Right and wrong, good and bad, POC, POD, all 9, shorts, boys, and beyonds®.***

What would you like your life to look like?

Awesome, this was day 1 of energy pull. Well done! You can continue pulling energy all day as and when you like as a way of getting familiar with the pull. Your being has been pulling energy for years now, you've just recognized that particular energy. Are you willing to have more of it?

Energy Pull 2

Pull energy from the front of you into you and out of you. Pull... Pull... What does it feel like to your body? Sense what your body is feeling.

If your body had to show up the way it would like to, what would it show up as? Get a sense of that. Let the awareness come to you. Now, put that energy in front of you and pull energy from the universe into that, into you and out of you. Pull..pull for as long as you like.

What energy, space and consciousness can you and your body be to be totally irrational for all eternity with total ease? ***Right and wrong, good and bad, pod and poc, all 9, shorts, boys and beyonds***®

What energy, space and consciousness can you and your body be to have total clarity with all of this for all eternity with total ease?

Energy Pull 3

Today pull the 5 elements of intimacy into your life. 5 elements of intimacy- honour, trust, vulnerability, allowance and gratitude.

Before you start to pull, flow energy to everything and everyone that is sucking you of your energy. Flow tsunamis of energy to them. More…More… Awesome! Now, pull energy from the universe into your body and out of your body. Now put your hands in front of you and perceive the energetic ball in your hands. Ask the universe to show you what honour looks like "Universe show me what honour for me looks like?". Honour is not the fake pride that exists in this reality. Honouring is to honour one without having the need to change them. Ask, "Universe show me what honour for me looks like?". Keep pulling. You can place that in the ball. Now, ask the universe to show you what honour for you looks like, "Universe show me what trusting me looks like?". Place that in the ball. Ask "Universe show me what vulnerability for me looks like?". Get a sense of that. Be with it. Now, place that in the ball. Vulnerability is not weakness. Vulnerability is being the open wound. Next, ask "Universe show me what allowance for me looks like?". Allowance is being in interesting point of view, where there's no alignment and agreement, no resistance and reaction. Everything is just a point of view- an interesting point of view, not right not wrong. There's nothing to prove. Get a sense of what that is for you. Place that in the ball. Ask "Universe show me what gratitude for me looks like?". In a space of gratitude there is no judgment. At one time either gratitude exists or judgment, both cannot co-exist at the same time. Place that in the ball too. Now see all 5 elements in the ball. Fill the ball up with energy, pull tsunamis of energy from the top into the ball, from the bottom, from the front and from the back. Pull.. pull… See the ball pulsating with energy. Is there any emp-ty space? Fill that too. Now pull tsunamis of energy from the universe into the ball, into you and out of you. Don't make it significant. Just pull. Pull.. You're awesome at this, don't let anyone tell you otherwise, even if it's you ;) Pull… Now send out trickles of energy to everyone, every being, every molecule of the universe that would contribute in actualizing this for you with total ease.

"ASK AND YOU SHALL RECEIVE"

What are you not asking for that if you would, would change all that is stuck with total ease?

***Right and wrong, good and bad, pod and poc, all 9, shorts, boys and beyonds**®*

Energy Pull 4

What have you decided you cannot be and will not be that if you would be it, would give you freedom from all that is holding you back? ***Right and wrong, good and bad, pod and poc, all 9, shorts, boys and beyonds**®*

Style your Life

Let's start with just pulling energy, pull, pull. Pull from everything and everyone that is asking for this pull. And no, you cannot deplete them of their energy. You are pulling the universe's energy not theirs ☺. Pull…

What energy, space and consciousness can you and your body be to have total clarity and ease with all of this for all eternity? ***Right and wrong, good and bad, pod and poc, all 9, shorts, boys and beyonds®.*** What would you like to actualize today my friends? What is it that you'd like to invite into your life?

What would you like to have in your life and as your life that you've decided is too big and too much? Ask for that!

How much money have you decided is a beyond? Where have you decided it has to come from? Pod and Poc that and are you willing to receive it wherever it's going to show up from?

What have you decided you would never create because in order to do that you would have to be an awful, vicious person? Are you willing to create that, let the how's, what's and what if's be. Are you willing to create that?

Place these 3 things in front of you.

What have you decided you cannot be and will not be that if you would be it, would give you freedom from all that is holding you back? ***Right and wrong, good and bad, pod and poc, all 9, shorts, boys and beyonds***. Pull energy from the universe, into them, into you and out of you. Pull. Pull tsunamis of energy. If you were truly being you, how would you pull energy? Continue to pull for as long as you like and then send trickles to everyone in the universe that will actualize this with total ease.

What energy, space and consciousness can you and your body be to create a reality totally beyond this reality with total ease?

Energy Pull 5

How much change are you willing to have? A little, a lot or megatons?

What will it take to have that change? Being rational or irrational?

Living in someone else's reality or creating your own?

Are you willing to create your own reality my beautiful beings?

Pull…

What if your very being was an energy pull?

Pull..

1-What would your body like to show up as?

2-What kind of clothes would your body like to wear?

3-Where would your body like to live?

4-Who would your body like to be around?

5-What future is your body asking to create?

Place these in front of you, in the energy ball. Pull energy from the universe, into the ball, fill it up with tsunamis of energy, from the top, bottom, left, right, center, everywhere. Let it pulsate with the energy. Now, pull energy from the front into the ball, through you and out of you. Pull… and send trickles back into the universe to every being that would like to contribute to actualizing this for you, in this reality with total ease.

This way, when they meet you, they'll know you, they'll have a connection with you already.

What energy, space and consciousness can you and your body be to be out of control, out of definition, out of concentricity, out of linearity, out of time, space and definition with total ease? *Right and wrong, good and bad, pod and poc, all 9, shorts, boys and beyonds®.*

You can create an energy pull for absolutely anything. For your business, your money flows, your travel, anything at all. Have fun with it. Don't be vested in the outcome and please don't have a timeframe in mind. Let the universe show you its magic.

Energy Pull 6

You can sit up, lie down or be however you would like to be. How much have you disconnected yourself from the earth? If you have your feet on the ground, ask for communion with earth to show up. Just ask "What energy, space and consciousness can my body and I be to be in communion with the earth with ease?".

The earth has no point of view, no significance. It doesn't judge us. Are you willing to see yourself from the eyes of the earth? How many jails are you using to create the dominance of e=mc square as the justification to create the comfortable distance between you and the earth are you choosing? Everything that is will you destroy and uncreate it all? ***Right and wrong, good and bad, POC, POD, all 9, shorts, boys, and beyonds.***

Are you willing to receive the contribution that the earth has to offer to actualizing all your creations?

What would you like your business to look like? Your business has a consciousness of its own, are you willing to hear what it's asking for? What does it require of you? Which part of your business requires your attention in this very moment? Put that in front of you.

Don't look for an answer, words are not needed. An energy is enough, even if you think you don't know what it is, every question brings up an energy. Be with that.

What is your business asking to create? What are you and your business willing to create together that you haven't asked for that if you would, would create a tsunami of possibility? Get an energy of what that is for you and place that in front of you.

Would you like your business to thrive? Who and what can show up that can contribute to making your business thrive, not survive. Get an energy of that and place that in front of you.

Your business has an energy of its own, your business and you are not one. Be willing to look at what it requires and desires. What you require and what it requires could be totally different.

Everywhere you have galumped you and your business as one, will you destroy and uncreate it all? ***Right and wrong, good and bad, POC, POD, all 9, shorts, boys, and beyonds®.***

Everywhere you are using causal incarceration as the backbone to your business, can you destroy and uncreate all that? ***Right and wrong, good and bad, POC, POD, all 9, shorts, boys, and beyonds®.***

Causal incarceration is when you believe that every cause has an effect. It's the prison that says cause and effect are the only source for anything, or they are the source for reality, and that every cause has to have an effect, and if you're going to create some effect, you have to have a previous cause, and that all the effects on your life are based on all the previous causes, rather than on what you can choose and what you can create. Everything that is will you destroy and uncreate all that? ***Right and wrong, good and bad, POC, POD, all 9, shorts, boys, and beyonds®.***

What could you change in your business, reality and life that if you were willing to change it would create more possibility, money than you have ever thought?

Right and wrong, good and bad, POC, POD, all 9, shorts, boys, and beyonds®.

Now pull energy through your asks, through you and out of you. Pull tsunamis of energy.

There is no right and wrong, just different. Your business is not right or wrong, just different.

Continue to pull as the clearings go on, as you read. Pull… Pull….Pull

And now send trickles back to everything and everyone that can actualize this for you in this reality with total ease.

When they meet you, they will already know you, they would want to contribute to you and receive from you. This might be what they have been asking for as well ;).

What else is possible® with your business that you've never imagined?

Energy Pull 7

Let's start with flowing every energy flow that is required in your world, in your universe. Every relationship, every being that is sucking you of your energy, flow tsunamis of energy to them. Don't make it significant. If you align and agree, or resist and react, it will have an effect on you but if you're willing to receive it without any point of view, it will just go through you and not stick to you.

Flow energy to everyone requiring a flow.

What kind of relationships would you like to style your life with? What kind of beings would you like to have in your life? What kind of bodies would your body like around it?

Would you like beings with bodies that are kind, that are nurturing, caring, who are happy to see you happy, who are happy to see you step into being greater, who you inspire as well as who inspire you to create greater? People who are an energy of gifting as well as receiving? What is it for you?

Put that in front of you.

Would you like to be more social? Would you like to have fun with people socializing? Would you like people to show up who can be fun to party with? If yes, ask for that. You can put that in front of you.

What energy, space and consciousness can you and your body be to be the social butterfly you truly be?

Everything that doesn't allow that to show up, can you destroy and uncreate that? ***Right and wrong, good and bad, POC, POD, all 9, shorts, boys, and beyonds®.***

Would you like the 5 elements of intimacy with and in your relationships? (5 elements of intimacy explained in pull 3). Place that in front of you.

Above all, are you willing to receive all of that with yourself? How much have you separated you from you? What have you defined you as that keeps you limited? How much comfortable distance are you using with yourself that creates you rejecting you in totality? Everything that is, ***Right and wrong, good and bad, POC, POD, all 9, shorts, boys, and beyonds®.***

What would the world be like if you were willing to care for you and honour you in the way you could honour you?

What jails are you using to create the dominance of e=mc square for the creation of comfortable distance between you and true caring are you choosing?

If you would receive you, what would that look like? Place that in front of you.

Pull, realize how even while we're asking these questions, you are continuously pulling energy. It doesn't require any doing or visualization. Pull through the universe, through your asks, into you, through you and out of you. Pull...pull...

Now send trickles to everyone in the universe that can contribute to actualizing your asks with total ease.

What energy, space and consciousness can you and your body be to create a reality with relationships totally beyond this reality with total ease? ***Right and wrong, good and bad, POC, POD, all 9, shorts, boys, and beyonds®.***

Energy Pull 8

Are you willing to ask for the energy of sexualness to contribute to you? Sexualness has nothing to do with copulation. Are you willing to ask for the healing, caring, nurturing, joyful, creative, generative, expansive and orgasmic energy to contribute to you? That is the energy of sexualness. What if you could ask for the energy of sexualness to show up in all your creations? The willingness to receive sexualness is the willingness to increase your receiving as well.

What have you made vital, valuable and real about being the doormat to sexualness that keeps you from being it in totality? *Right and wrong, good and bad, POC, POD, all 9, shorts, boys, and beyonds®.*

Now, start pulling energy. Pull from the universe into your body and out of your body.

How much sexualness can you instill with and in your business, how much sexualness would you have to instill with your body to create a communion with it instead of rejecting it? Whenever you're willing to be the sexual energy (whatever it shows up as for you), people around you find you irresistible because sexualness is also a space of no judgment.

So, every time you meet a client for work, are you willing to be the energy of sexualness they can receive? *Right and wrong, good and bad, POC, POD, all 9, shorts, boys, and beyonds®.*

Also, let me ask you a question, when you are being the energy of sexualness, are you or are you not also changing things in people's universes as well?

I know when I'm being it, people are willing to receive from me and it instills a world of kindness in their reality as well. It shows them a possibility of a totally different reality, a reality beyond unkindness.

Put all this in front of you, whatever you're asking for. Put the energy of sexualness in front of you and now pull from the universe, into that into you and out of your body.

Pull...Pull...

If you feel a resistance coming up, ask a question "What am I unwilling to receive and be that if I would be it would create greater with total ease?"

Pull...Pull..

Now, send trickles out to everyone in the universe that can contribute to actualizing this for you with total ease. This would create greater for them as well, if they are willing to receive it.

How much fun can you have being the energy of you?

Energy Pull 9

What adventure is life that you haven't yet allowed it to be?

Everything that stops the intensive adventure of living - family, time, work will you destroy and uncreate it all? ***Right and wrong, good and bad, POC, POD, all 9, shorts, boys, and beyonds®.***

What have you decided is the "way of life" that has you stuck in the pile of poo rather than the adventure of living? ***Right and wrong, good and bad, POC, POD, all 9, shorts, boys, and beyonds®.***

What is the energy of adventure for you? Everywhere you bought into the lies of the limitations of adventure can you destroy and uncreate that? ***Right and wrong, good and bad, POC, POD, all 9, shorts, boys, and beyonds®.***

How nurtured are you willing to be? If you were willing to be nurtured, would the adventure of living be greater?

What if you were willing to be totally nurtured? Would you be willing to be totally nourished by the universe, by the planet, by people around you?

Everything that doesn't allow that to show up, can you destroy and uncreate it all? ***Right and wrong, good and bad, POC, POD, all 9, shorts, boys, and beyonds®.***

Pull.. Keep pulling….

What if you were willing to be totally nurtured? Would you be willing to be totally nourished by the universe, by the planet, by people around you?

What adventure is life that you haven't yet allowed it to be?

Now, pull from the universe, pull from these into you and out of you. Please feel free to add to remove any of the asks. This is your playground, create it your way.

Pull…Pull…

And now send trickles into the universe.

What else is possible® my friends?

Energy Pull 10

What future are the choices that you are making today creating?

What are you unwilling to be that if you would be it would actualize a greater future with total ease?

What choices could you make that would actualize all that you desire with total ease?

What future are the choices you are making today creating?

What can you pull today to allow this to show up faster than 10 years?

Pull.. pull from the universe into you and out of you.

What if your being is an energy puller, at all times?

What energy, space and consciousness can you and your body be to outcreate everything you've created so far with total ease? ***Right and wrong, good and bad, POC, POD, all 9, shorts, boys, and beyonds®.***

My beautiful friends, you can continue using the pulls to actualize anything and everything you desire. You can do a pull for a minute, 10 minutes, 30 minutes, whatever you like.

This is your playground. Create it your way.

What are the energy pulls for you?

P.S. Big thank you Julia for introducing me to this magical world of energy pulls. Anything is truly possible!!!!

Chapter 10

On Colours

"THE BEST COLOUR IN THE WHOLE WORLD IS THE ONE THAT LOOKS GOOD ON YOU".

Coco Chanel

Colours have a way of adding life. Each colour has something to say, something to contribute.

At any point of time, is it possible that you stopped showering yourself with colours in life? Would you like to change that?

What lies, whose lies and how many lies are you using to live the colourless life you are choosing? Everything that is will you destroy and uncreate it all?

***Right and wrong, good and bad, POC, POD, all 9,
shorts, boys, and beyonds®.***

Are you ready to invite them in?

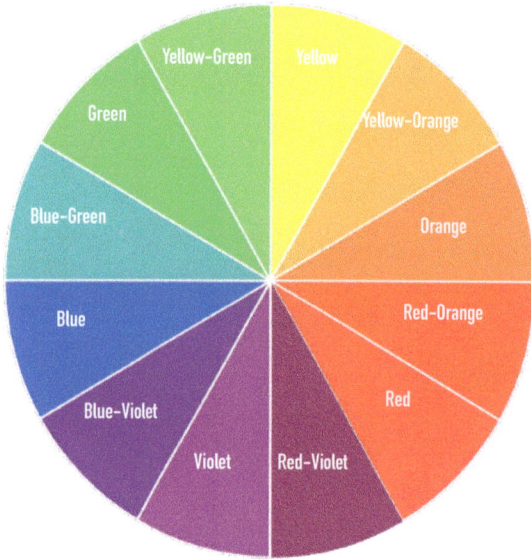

This is a basic colour wheel that'll help you make colour
choices. We've all studied these in school but here's a
quick refresher of the colours in case you've forgotten
it. Red, blue and yellow are primary colours. When you
mix red and yellow, you get orange; mix blue and yel-

low, you get green; mix red and blue, you get violet. Orange, green and violet are hence called secondary colours. Tertiary colours like red-violet and blue-violet are derived by mixing a primary colour with a secondary colour.

Primary Colours: Yellow, Red and Blue

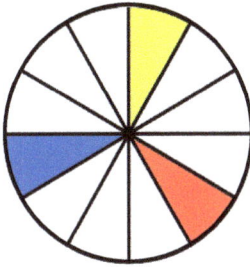

Secondary Colours: Orange, Purple and Green

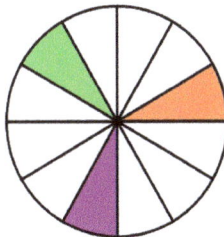

Tertiary Colours: Yellow Orange, Red Orange, Red Violet, Blue- Violet, Blue- green, Yellow Green

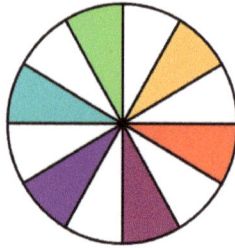

Analogues: Analogous colours are any three colours next to each other on the wheel. For example, orange, yellow-orange, and yellow.

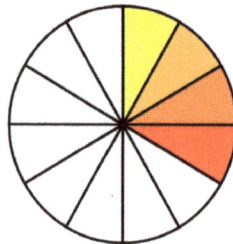

Complementary: Complementary colours are any two colours opposite each other on the wheel. For example, blue and orange, or red and green, yellow and violet. These create a high contrast, so use them when you want something to stand out.

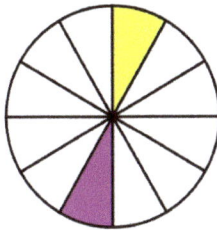

Split- Complementary: Split complementary colours use three colours. The scheme takes one colour and matches it with the two colours adjacent to its complementary colour. For example, blue, yellow-orange and red-orange.

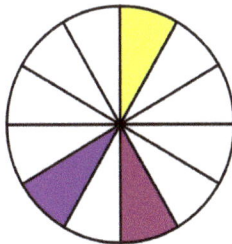

Warm Colours and Cool Colours

Warm colours represent passion, happiness, enthusiasm, energy. Cool colours represent a sense of calm and professionalism.

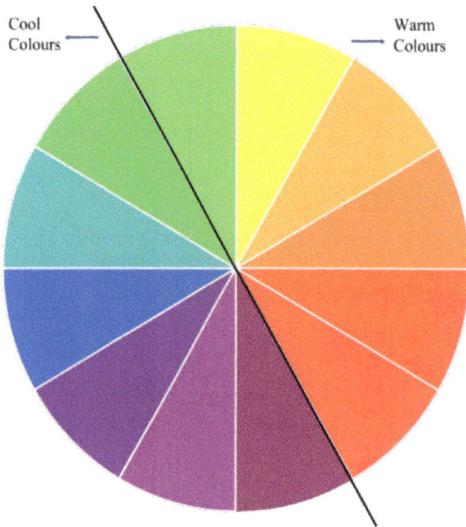

Now, you have a basic sense of colour theory. Let's apply it to your wardrobe now, shall we? Take a photocopy of the colour wheel and stick it to your wardrobe's door. The next time you pick out one clothing item, just refer to the chart to see what colours in your closet will best complement it; and use the basics of warm and cool colours to convey the emotion you want to project.

As a very interesting point of view, you may or may not want to have more than three colours in your outfit. Try different colours against your skin and learn which palettes look best on you. Talk to your body and ask it to guide you and show you what it would like to wear, what combinations it would like to put on.

Useful tip: Don't be scared. Paint is not permanent; you can always change it ;)

References for colours

Now, let's not own and buy into these, rather let's use these to tap into the worlds of others. The idea is not to make these definitions real and significant for ourselves so we can create beyond them. The idea is to use and create a persona with these colours so others can see us as something they've decided about colours and use it to create greater for everyone involved. You can choose to wear red and carry off the definition of a blue. These colours do not define who you be, they are just a tool to use.

Red- Red is the colour of blood. So, it tends to be associated with energy, war, danger strength, power, determination as well as passion, power and love.

Light red represents joy, sexuality, passion, sensitivity, and love. **Pink** denotes feminine qualities and passiveness.

Dark red is associated with vigour, willpower, rage, anger, leadership, courage, longing, malice, and wrath.

Brown suggests stability and denotes masculine qualities.

Reddish-brown is associated with harvest and fall.

Yellow- Yellow can be related to sunshine. It is associated with joy, happiness, intellect and energy. Yellow tends to have a warming effect, it brings up a cheerful and happy energy. Bright yellow is an attention getter. At the same time, you don't want to over do the yellow. I personally love yellow when paired with white during the days. You can also use yellow as an accessory to add a dash of colour.

Dull (dingy) yellow represents caution, decay, sickness.

Light yellow is associated with intellect, freshness, and joy.

Blue- Blue is the colour of the sky and the sea. It is often associated with depth and stability. It could stand for trust, loyalty, wisdom, confidence, intelligence. Blue is also related to consciousness and intellect.

Light blue is associated with health, healing, tranquility, understanding, and softness.

Dark blue represents knowledge, power, integrity, and seriousness.

Orange- Orange combines the energy of red and the happiness of yellow. It is associated with joy, sunshine, and the tropics. Orange represents enthusiasm, fascination, happiness, creativity, determination, attraction, success, encouragement and stimulation.

Red-orange corresponds to desire, sexual passion, pleasure, domination, aggression, and thirst for action.

Gold evokes the feeling of prestige. The meaning of gold is illumination, wisdom, and wealth. Gold often symbolizes high quality.

Green- Green is the colour of nature. It symbolizes growth, harmony, freshness, and fertility. Green has strong emotional correspondence with safety. Green is considered to have a great healing power. Green suggests stability and endurance.

Yellow-green can indicate sickness.

Aqua is associated with emotional healing and protection.

Olive green is the traditional colour of peace.

Purple- Purple combines the stability of blue and the energy of red. Purple is associated with royalty. It symbolizes power, nobility, luxury and ambition. It conveys wealth and extravagance. Purple is associated with wisdom, dignity, independence, creativity, mystery, and magic. According to surveys, almost 75 percent of pre-adolescent children prefer purple to all other colours. Purple is a very rare colour in nature; some people consider it to be artificial.

Light purple evokes romantic and nostalgic feelings.

White- White is associated with light, goodness, innocence, purity, and virginity. It is considered to be the colour of perfection. White means safety, purity, and cleanliness. White usually has a positive connotation. White can represent a successful beginning. Angels are usually imagined wearing white clothes. White is also associated with hospitals, doctors, and sterility too. How would you like to use it?

Black- Black is associated with power, elegance, formality, death, evil, and mystery. Black denotes strength and authority, it is considered to be a very formal, elegant, and prestigious colour. Black gives the feeling of perspective and depth. Black contrasts well with bright colours. A black suit or dress can make you look thinner.

So, everywhere we have made these colours significant can you destroy and uncreate it all? ***Right and wrong, good and bad, POC, POD, all 9, shorts, boys, and beyonds®.***

If you buy into this, you will create your reality based on it. It wont be your reality! Be willing to sell it, not buy it ;)

You can wear one colour and have attributes of them all, if you choose!

Chapter 11

Handy Tips

"DON'T BE INTO TRENDS. DON'T MAKE
FASHION OWN YOU, BUT YOU DECIDE
WHAT YOU ARE, WHAT YOU WANT TO
EXPRESS BY THE WAY YOU DRESS AND THE
WAY YOU LIVE."

Gianni Versace

These are just fun suggestions to play with, follow your
knowing to create what's fun for you and your body.

Tools To Use While Shopping

Get present with your body. Feel your feet on the ground. Ask for restoration of communion with earth to run.

Communicate with your body, ask questions. You can start with- body where would you like to go shopping today?

Ask your body to show up stores that would be nurturing, fun and expansive.

Please follow your knowing (airy, breezy, light) is your knowing. Remember anything that has a but in it has a lie attached to it!

Everything is the opposite of what it appears to be and nothing is the opposite of what it appears to be.

Ask your body, "Body what would you feel wealthy in?"

Ask the clothes, "If I buy you, will you make me money?"

Be willing to tap into the future and ask "What would my life be like if I bought this?". Every item has an energy that you invite into your life and living.

Style your Life

If your body gets a yes for a certain outfit, cosmetic, jewellery etc and your mind tells you thousands of reasons why it wont look good, run "Whose lies, what lies and how many lies am I using to create this point of *view am I choosing?*"

Above all, just have fun exploring all the various energies that are there, pull energy from everything you perceive as wealthy and nurturing and invite it into your life!

Happy Shopping ☺

Chapter 12

Styling Your Future

"FASHION IS NOT NECESSARILY ABOUT
LABELS. IT'S NOT ABOUT BRANDS. IT'S
ABOUT SOMETHING ELSE THAT COMES
FROM WITHIN YOU."

Ralph Lauren

What energy, space and consciousness can you and your body be to be totally irrational with your choices that would create a future totally beyond this reality with total ease? Everything that is will you destroy and un-create it all? **Right and wrong, good and bad, POC, POD, all 9, shorts, boys, and beyonds®.**

Being willing to have an irrational future is willing to create a completely unpredictable future, not based on what others have projected at you, not based on what is expected of you, not based on what you expect out of yourself. It is a space where you are willing to choose whatever will create greater.

Irrational creates sanity, rational justifies insanity.

How much fun can you have creating a future that is styled by you?

That too is an irrational point of view.

Are you willing to trust you and know that you know what will create greater for you? We've spent most of our lives looking for answers outside of us, looking for someone who is greater than us to tell us what will work for us.

Are you willing to acknowledge now that you are the greatness you've been looking for? It's not outside of you.

We've spent days looking at colour forecasts and different fashion forecasts and fashion shows to know what is "in", which is not wrong. It's great to educate ourselves on all of that but are you willing to actually explore what works for you not based on what the forecast said but based on what your body asked for? Are you willing to care and nurture for your body the way you hoped and expected someone else to?

What if you could style your life, your future according to what works for you in that very moment? You know how molecules are changing every second, you as a being are changing every second, your body changes every second. So, when energies are changing every second, allow your choices to change too. Any awareness of a choice when "decided" that it works for you becomes a judgment and becomes solid and a limitation. Be willing to ask a question after every awareness. The second you decide that it is the right way of being and doing things, it becomes a huge limitation.

Being willing to be in 10 second increments is the willingness to be irrational.

Be willing to outcreate every success of yours. Every time you decide that you've achieved something great and you decide that it can't get better, ask another question! What else is possible®? There is nothing that is the greatest, it's just different. Two creations can never be the same, they both can create the greatest in their own ways at the same time not being greater than one another. My beautiful friends, how much fun can you have now styling your life, designing your life according to what works for you?

A Few Abbreviations

Jails- Judgments, Agendas, Inventions and Lies.

E=MC Square (E=Mc2)– Evil=Mediocrity Times Corruption.

WWIT-What will it take?

WEIP-What else is possible®?

HDIGABTT- How does it get any better than this?®

All Clearings

All the definitions you've given to partying can you destroy and uncreate that?" ***Right and wrong, good and bad, pod and poc, all 9, shorts, boys and beyonds®.***

Are you willing to ask for that to show up? Everything that doesn't allow that can we destroy and uncreate that? ***Right and wrong, good and bad, pod and poc, all 9, shorts, boys and beyonds®.***

What lies, whose lies and how many lies are you using to create mourning your life you are choosing? ***Right and wrong, good and bad, pod and poc, all 9, shorts, boys and beyonds®.***

Everything you have done to make yourself wrong and less to make others greater even though you knew you weren't wrong will you destroy and uncreate that? ***Right and wrong, good and bad, pod and poc, all 9, shorts, boys and beyonds®.***

Whose lies, what lies and how many lies are you using to justify being wrong are you choosing?

Right and wrong, good and bad, pod and poc, all 9, shorts, boys and beyonds®.

What lies, whose lies and how many lies am I using to create this as my reality am I choosing? **Right and wrong, good and bad, pod and poc, all 9, shorts, boys and beyonds®.**

How many definitions of you have you created that are actually creating the limitation of you? Everything that is times a godzillion will you destroy and uncreate it all? **Right and wrong, good and bad, pod and poc, all 9, shorts, boys and beyonds®.**

Whose lies and what lies and how many lies are you using to create you based on all the definitions of your name are you choosing? **Right and wrong, good and bad, pod and poc, all 9, shorts, boys and beyonds®.**

Everywhere you have misidentified and misapplied you as your name and your name as you can you now destroy and uncreate it? **Right and wrong, good and bad, pod and poc, all 9, shorts, boys and beyonds®.**

All the oaths, vows, commealties, fealties, commitments, binding and bonding contracts you have to be your name and only your name for all eternity, can you now revoke, recant, rescind, reclaim, renounce, denounce, destroy and uncreate it all? ***Right and wrong, good and bad, pod and poc, all 9, shorts, boys and beyonds®.***

Are you willing to destroy all these identities you have created? ***Right and wrong, good and bad, all 9, POD, POC, shorts, boys and beyonds®.***

How many jails are you using as the dominance of e=mc square as the justification of your identity are you choosing? ***Right and wrong, good and bad, all 9, POD, POC, shorts, boys and beyonds®.***

Are you willing to be so irrational in every moment that the universe is seduced to provide everything you require with total ease? Everything that doesn't allow that, will you destroy and uncreate it all? ***Right and wrong, good and bad, all 9, POD, POC, shorts, boys and beyonds®.***

How many jails are you using as the dominance of e=mc square as the justification of being rational are you choosing? ***Right and wrong, good and bad, all 9, POD, POC, shorts, boys and beyonds®.***

How many jails are you using as the dominance of e=mc square as the justification of fear of change are you choosing? *Right and wrong, good and bad, all 9, POD, POC, shorts, boys and beyonds®.*

Whose lies, what lies and how many faux beingnesses are you using to create the constant you are choosing?

Right and wrong, good and bad, all 9, POD, POC, shorts, boys and beyonds®.

How much change are you willing to receive and have? *Right and wrong, good and bad, all 9, POD, POC, shorts, boys and beyonds®.*

How many points of view are you using to spin awarenesses and possibilities into judgments are you choosing? Everything that is will you destroy and un-create it all? *Right and wrong, good and bad, all 9, POD, POC, shorts, boys and beyonds®.*

How many JAILS are you using to create the dominance of E=mc2 as the creation of your future from fixed points of view, fixed realities, fixed beingnesses, fixed thoughts, feelings and emotions and fixed lies that keeps you from creating beyond the limitations you've defined as you? *Right and wrong, good and bad, all 9, POD, POC, shorts, boys and beyonds®.*

All of your past experience, everything you've created in the past 6 months that you've decided defines the next 6 months can you destroy and uncreate that? ***Right and wrong, good and bad, all 9, POD, POC, shorts, boys and beyonds®.***

How much do we all spurn ourselves, reject ourselves just so we can carry forward the decision we made years back or a while ago as though that proves a rightness? Everything that is can you destroy and uncreate that please? ***Right and wrong, good and bad, all 9, POD, POC, shorts, boys and beyonds®.***

What jails are you using to create the dominance of e=mc2 as only spurning others to have and maintain the rightness of you and your choices are you choosing? ***Right and wrong, good and bad, pod and poc, all 9, shorts, boys and beyonds®***

What jails are you using to create the dominance of e=mc2 as only spurning yourself to have and maintain the rightness of you and your choices are you choosing? ***Right and wrong, good and bad, pod and poc, all 9, shorts, boys and beyonds®.***

Everywhere you have misidentified and misapplied power as not the potency it is and everything you've done to call yourself powerless when what you are really doing is creating impotence. Revoke, recant, rescind, reclaim, renounce, denounce, destroy and uncreate all of this? *Right and wrong, good and bad, pod, poc, all 9, shorts, boys, and beyonds*®.

What potency are you refusing with the impotence you are choosing? Everything that is will you, revoke, recant, rescind, reclaim, renounce, denounce, destroy and uncreate all of this? *Right, Wrong, Good, Bad, POD, POC, All 9, shorts, boys, and beyonds*®.

What being are you avoiding with the impotence you are choosing? Everything that is will you, revoke, recant, rescind, reclaim, renounce, denounce, destroy and uncreate all of this? *Right, Wrong, Good, Bad, POD, POC, All 9, shorts, boys, and beyonds*®.

What bastardization of infinite power and potency are you using to create the pathetic pile of shit life you are choosing? Everything that is times a godzillion will you destroy and uncreate it all? *Right and wrong, good and bad, pod and poc, all 9, shorts, boys and beyonds*®.

Everything you have done to buy proving as your point of view, can you destroy and uncreate it please? *Right and wrong, good and bad, pod and poc, all 9, shorts, boys and beyonds*®.

Everything that you've defined power as, can you destroy and uncreate it please? ***Right and wrong, good and bad, pod and poc, all 9, shorts, boys and beyonds®.***

All the definitions, judgments, separations, rejections, conclusions you have about beauty can you destroy and uncreate that please? ***Right and wrong, good and bad, pod and poc, all 9, shorts, boys and beyonds®.***

Whose lies, what lies and how many faux beingnesses are you using to create the beautiful you are choosing? ***Right and wrong, good and bad, pod and poc, all 9, shorts, boys and beyonds®.***

Are you willing to let go of the lies you bought from others as to what beauty is and let that which is true for you to show up? Everything that doesn't allow that can you destroy and uncreate it? ***Right and wrong, good and bad, pod and poc, all 9, shorts, boys and beyonds®.***

What have you invented as beauty? Everything that is will you destroy and uncreate it all? ***Right and wrong, good and bad, POC, POD, all 9, shorts, boys, and beyonds®.***

What have you invented as not beauty? Everything that is will you destroy and uncreate it all? *Right and wrong, good and bad, POC, POD, all 9, shorts, boys, and beyonds®.*

Everywhere you bought into the lie that beauty is expensive can you destroy and uncreate that? *Right and wrong, good and bad, POC, POD, all 9, shorts, boys, and beyonds®.*

Everywhere you've decided you will only be a lady when you reach a certain peak of wealth, will you destroy and uncreate it all? *Right and wrong, good and bad, POC, POD, all 9, shorts, boys, and beyonds®.*

What have you defined as being a lady that keeps you rejecting the lady you truly be? *Right and wrong, good and bad, POC, POD, all 9, shorts, boys, and beyonds®.*

What if you already are being a lady and just haven't acknowledged it because its always been? Everything that is, will you destroy and uncreate it all? *Right and wrong, good and bad, POC, POD, all 9, shorts, boys, and beyonds®.*

Everything you've done to buy into the point of view that your body is wrong and it must be separated, can you destroy and uncreate it all? ***Right and wrong, good and bad, POC, POD, all 9, shorts, boys, and beyonds®.***

What religious and spiritual point of view are you using to create your body are you choosing? ***Right and wrong, good and bad, POC, POD, all 9, shorts, boys, and beyonds®.***

How many jails (judgments, agendas, inventions and lies) are you using to create the domination of E=mc2 (Evil, mediocrity and corruption) as always trying to use your rational mind and your rational conclusions rather than your irrational awareness that keeps you from the joy of having, being, doing creating and generating your body beyond your wildest dreams. ***Right and wrong, good and bad, POC, POD, all 9, shorts, boys, and beyonds®.***

How many jails are you using to create the dominance of E=mc2 as the creation of sexualness from fixed points of view, fixed realities, fixed beingnesses, fixed thoughts, feelings and emotions, and fixed lies that keeps you from creating beyond the limitations you've defined as real that are not? ***Right and wrong, good and bad, POC, POD, all 9, shorts, boys, and beyonds®.***

What jails are you using to create the dominance of e=mc square as the fixed points of view, fixed lies, fixed realities, feelings and emotions, form, structure and significance, fixed beingnesses for making you wrong in totality with and for having physical reality? ***Right and wrong, good and bad, POC, POD, all 9, shorts, boys, and beyonds®.***

If your body got the future that it desired, how much greater would it be than the future you've decided? Everything you've done to invalidate all of that, will you destroy and uncreate it? ***Right and wrong, good and bad, POC, POD, all 9, shorts, boys, and beyonds®.***

Whose lies and what lies are you using to avoid the awareness of your body's desires are you choosing? ***Right and wrong, good and bad, POC, POD, all 9, shorts, boys, and beyonds®.***

How many jails are you using to create the dominance of E=mc2 as the justification of creation of your body as a limitation are you choosing? ***Right and wrong, good and bad, POC, POD, all 9, shorts, boys, and beyonds®.***

Whose lies, what lies and how many lies are you using that keeps you from being the phenomenance of conscious embodiment of you, you are choosing? ***Right*** *and wrong, good and bad, POD, POC, all 9, shorts, boys, and beyonds®.*

Whose lies, what lies and how many lies are you using that has you creating the finiteness of embodiment you are choosing? *Right and wrong, good and bad, POD, POC, all 9, shorts, boys, and beyonds®.*

Whose lies, what lies and how many lies are you using that keeps you from accessing and embodying all energies? *Right and wrong, good and bad, POD, POC, all 9, shorts, boys, and beyonds®.*

How many jails are you using as the dominance of e=mc square as the justification of embodiment of this reality are you choosing? *Right and wrong, good and bad, pod and poc, all 9, shorts, boys and beyonds®.*

What have you made so vital, valuable and real about human mechanistic embodiment that keeps you from the joyful, playful, creative, expansive ease of humanoid embodiment that you and your body are here to create and be? *Right and wrong, good and bad, pod and poc, all 9, shorts, boys and beyonds®.*

How much judgment are you using to make sure your body cannot receive the joy of the food and drink you are choosing? *Right and wrong, good and bad, pod and poc, all 9, shorts, boys and beyonds®.*

Whose dietary scale of insanity are you eating from? ***Right and wrong, good and bad, pod and poc, all 9, shorts, boys and beyonds®.***

Everything you've done to justify all the body shapes as reality can you destroy and uncreate that? ***Right and wrong, good and bad, POC, POD, all 9, shorts, boys, and beyonds®.***

How much have you decided you have to only have the "abundant things" on days people are there to see? Are you willing to be this energy with yourself? Everything that is will you destroy and uncreate it all? ***Right and wrong, good and bad, POC, POD, all 9, shorts, boys, and beyonds®.***

Are you willing to be honor, trust, gratitude, allowance, vulnerability with abundant living? Everything that is will you destroy and uncreate it all? ***Right and wrong, good and bad, POC, POD, all 9, shorts, boys, and beyonds®.***

How much have you decided you have to hide all the "abundant things" on days people are there to see? Are you willing to be this energy with yourself at all times? Everything that is will you destroy and uncreate it all? ***Right and wrong, good and bad, POC, POD, all 9, shorts, boys, and beyonds®.***

What lies, whose lies, how many lies are you using to resist and reject the abundance of you, you truly be? Everything that is will you destroy and uncreate it all? ***Right and wrong, good and bad, POC, POD, all 9, shorts, boys, and beyonds***

Are you willing to let abundance and wealth know you would like to actually have it or are you busy living the pathetic life pretending you're working your ass off to "earn" money and have wealth one day? Is that one day going to come? Nope, when that one day arrives it'll be "today", not good enough for you. ;)

So, everything you've done to throw all your todays away in hope of your one day can you destroy and un-create that? ***Right and wrong, good and bad, POC, POD, all 9, shorts, boys, and beyonds®.***

Everything you've done/ this reality has done for you to believe that money is the creative force and source that you need will you destroy and uncreate it? ***Right and wrong, good and bad, POC, POD, all 9, shorts, boys, and beyonds®.***

Are you willing to be the voice of wealth and possibilities?

Everything you've done to buy into the lies of how much it takes to dress as a wealthy person can you destroy and uncreate that? ***Right and wrong, good and bad, POC, POD, all 9, shorts, boys, and beyonds®.***

What have you decided is loud, flashy, obnoxious, arrogant, shallow? Everything that is will you destroy and uncreate it? ***Right and wrong, good and bad, POC, POD, all 9, shorts, boys, and beyonds®.***

Whose lies, what lies and how many beingnesses are you using to create the sophistication, elegance and glamour you are choosing? Everything that is will you destroy and uncreate it? ***Right and wrong, good and bad, POC, POD, all 9, shorts, boys, and beyonds®.***

Everywhere we were told we are being materialistic every time we looked at something beautiful and wanted it, will you destroy and uncreate it all? ***Right and wrong, good and bad, POC, POD, all 9, shorts, boys, and beyonds®.***

Whose point of view are you doing interesting point of view from? Is it even yours? ***Right and wrong, good and bad, POC, POD, all 9, shorts, boys, and beyonds®.***

Everything you've done to resist the judgments thrown at you each time you choose to show up as you, can you destroy and uncreate that? ***Right and wrong, good and bad, pod and poc, all 9, shorts, boys and beyonds®.***

Whose lies, what lies and how many lies are you using to create the necessity of, and resistance of popularity and stardom are you choosing? ***Right and wrong, good and bad, pod and poc, all 9, shorts, boys and beyonds®.***

What will it take for you to be the social butterfly you truly be? Everything that doesn't allow that, will you destroy and uncreate it all? ***Right and wrong, good and bad, pod and poc, all 9, shorts, boys and beyonds®.***

What energy, space and consciousness can you and your body be to acknowledge your potency with total ease? ***Right and wrong, good and bad, POC, POD, all 9, shorts, boys, and beyonds®.***

What energy, space and consciousness can you and your body be to know, be, perceive, receive all of the energy pulls with total ease? ***Right and wrong, good and bad, POC, POD, all 9, shorts, boys, and beyonds®.***

What energy, space and consciousness can you and your body be to be totally irrational for all eternity with total ease? ***Right and wrong, good and bad, pod and poc, all 9, shorts, boys and beyonds®.***

What are you not asking for that if you would, would change all that is stuck with total ease?

Right and wrong, good and bad, pod and poc, all 9, shorts, boys and beyonds®.

What have you decided you cannot be and will not be that if you would be it, would give you freedom from all that is holding you back? **Right and wrong, good and bad, pod and poc, all 9, shorts, boys and beyonds®.**

What energy, space and consciousness can you and your body be to have total clarity and ease with all of this for all eternity? **Right and wrong, good and bad, pod and poc, all 9, shorts, boys and beyonds®.**

What have you decided you cannot be and will not be that if you would be it, would give you freedom from all that is holding you back? **Right and wrong, good and bad, pod and poc, all 9, shorts, boys and beyonds®.**

What energy, space and consciousness can you and your body be to be out of control, out of definition, out of concentricity, out of linearity, out of time, space and definition with total ease? **Right and wrong, good and bad, pod and poc, all 9, shorts, boys and beyonds®.**

The earth has no point of view, no significance. It doesn't judge us. Are you willing to see yourself from the eyes of the earth? How many jails are you using to create the dominance of e=mc square as the justification to create the comfortable distance between you and the earth are you choosing? Everything that is will you destroy and uncreate it all? ***Right and wrong, good and bad, POC, POD, all 9, shorts, boys, and beyonds®.***

Everywhere you have galumped you and your business as one, will you destroy and uncreate it all? ***Right and wrong, good and bad, POC, POD, all 9, shorts, boys, and beyonds®.***

Everywhere you are using causal incarceration as the backbone to your business, can you destroy and uncreate all that? ***Right and wrong, good and bad, POC, POD, all 9, shorts, boys, and beyonds®.***

What could you change in your business, reality and life that if you were willing to change it would create more possibility, money than you have ever thought? ***Right and wrong, good and bad, POC, POD, all 9, shorts, boys, and beyonds®.***

What energy, space and consciousness can you and your body be to be the social butterfly you truly be? Everything that doesn't allow that to show up, can you destroy and uncreate that? *Right and wrong, good and bad, POC, POD, all 9, shorts, boys, and beyonds®.*

How much have you separated you from you? What have you defined you as that keeps you limited? How much comfortable distance are you using with yourself that creates you rejecting you in totality? Everything that is, *Right and wrong, good and bad, POC, POD, all 9, shorts, boys, and beyonds®.*

What energy, space and consciousness can you and your body be to create a reality with relationships totally beyond this reality with total ease? *Right and wrong, good and bad, POC, POD, all 9, shorts, boys, and beyonds®.*

What have you made vital, valuable and real about being the doormat to sexualness that keeps you from being it in totality? *Right and wrong, good and bad, POC, POD, all 9, shorts, boys, and beyonds®.*

Every time you meet a client for work, are you willing to be the energy of sexualness they can receive? *Right and wrong, good and bad, POC, POD, all 9, shorts, boys, and beyonds®.*

Everything that stops the intensive adventure of living - family, time, work will you destroy and uncreate it all?

Right and wrong, good and bad, POC, POD, all 9, shorts, boys, and beyonds®.

What have you decided is the "way of life" that has you stuck in the pile of poo rather than the adventure of living? ***Right and wrong, good and bad, POC, POD, all 9, shorts, boys, and beyonds®.***

What is the energy of adventure for you? Everywhere you bought into the lies of the limitations of adventure can you destroy and uncreate that? ***Right and wrong, good and bad, POC, POD, all 9, shorts, boys, and beyonds®.***

What if you were willing to be totally nurtured? Would you be willing to be totally nourished by the universe, by the planet, by people around you?

Everything that doesn't allow that to show up, can you destroy and uncreate it all? ***Right and wrong, good and bad, POC, POD, all 9, shorts, boys, and beyonds®.***

What energy, space and consciousness can you and your body be to outcreate everything you've created so far with total ease? ***Right and wrong, good and bad, POC, POD, all 9, shorts, boys, and beyonds®.***

What energy, space and consciousness can you and your body be to be totally irrational with your choices that would create a future totally beyond this reality with total ease? Everything that is will you destroy and uncreate it all? ***Right and wrong, good and bad, POC, POD, all 9, shorts, boys, and beyonds®.***

About The Author

Isha Bawa is an Access Consciousness® Certified Facilitator and a Right Body For You Facilitator who lives in New Delhi, and empowers people around the world using the tools of Access Consciousness®.

She is someone who has always seen the sparkles of life, always seeing life from a different perspective.

She has clients all over the world and has empowered people to create beyond depression, anxiety, abuse, money problems, self-esteem challenges and many more.

Prior to this, she studied (Hons.) Fashion Business Management for 4 years at Pearl Academy of Fashion in New Delhi and studied at Heriott- Watt University in Edinburgh, Scotland as a part of her 4 years at college.

She has a different take on life and living and believes in thriving and showering possibilities and change into various people's worlds just by being. Her target is to create a world without separation, where people are empowered to embrace their true beauty and kindness.

Hi I'm Isha, You can find me in tons of different ways. I have listed some of them below-

Website: www.ishabawa.com

E-mail Address: ishabawa29@gmail.com

Facebook Profile: Isha Bawa

Facebook Page: Isha Bawa- Whispers Of Magical Possibilities

Instagram: Isha Bawa

Youtube: Isha Bawa

Right Body for You Facilitator

You can find out more about Access Consciousness® at www.accessconsciousness.com

About Access Consciousness®

Access Consciousness® has been created by Gary Douglas and co-created by Dr. Dain Heer and is available in more than 170 countries and has contributed to changing the lives of tens of thousands of people around the world for the past 30 years. Delivered through seminars, teleseries, books, audios and consultations, what most people love about it is that it actually works!

Access Consciousness offers you the tools and questions to create everything you desire in a different and easier way, and to change the things in your life that you haven't been able to change until now. It empowers you to know that you know and provides you with ways to become totally aware and to begin to function as the conscious being you truly are.

Style your Life

When you're willing to follow your knowing, and ask a question, it could be the one thing that unlocks your whole world! Are you ready for that?

DR DAIN HEER

These life-changing techniques, tools and processes are designed to empower you to create the life you desire. Practical, dynamic, and pragmatic, it provides step-by-step processes to facilitate you in being more conscious in every day life and eliminate all the barriers you have put up to receiving. Then life becomes an adventure of what would I like to choose? What would I like to create? How much fun can I have being alive?

ISHA BAWA

(Taken from https://www.accessconsciousness.com/en/
about/what-is-access-consciousness/)

You can find more information on
www.accessconsciousness.com

GARY DOUGLAS

Dr. DAIN HEER